Cambridge Opera Handbooks

Giacomo Puccini
Tosca

An illustration by the designer of the first *Tosca*, F. A. von Hohenstein, which appeared on posters and early vocal scores of the opera

Giacomo Puccini

Tosca

MOSCO CARNER

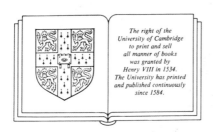

The right of the
University of Cambridge
to print and sell
all manner of books
was granted by
Henry VIII in 1534.
The University has printed
and published continuously
since 1584.

CAMBRIDGE UNIVERSITY PRESS

Cambridge
London   New York   New Rochelle
Melbourne   Sydney

Published by the Press Syndicate of the University of Cambridge
The Pitt Building, Trumpington Street, Cambridge CB2 1RP
32 East 57th Street, New York, NY 10022, USA
10 Stamford Road, Oakleigh, Melbourne 3166, Australia

First published 1985

Printed in Great Britain
at the University Press, Cambridge

Library of Congress catalogue card number: 84-23910

British Library Cataloguing in Publication Data

Carner, Mosco
Giacomo Puccini, Tosca. – (Cambridge Opera handbooks)
1. Puccini, Giacomo
1. Title
782.1′092′4 ML410.P89

ISBN 0 521 22824 7 hard covers
ISBN 0 521 29661 7 paperback

ME

CAMBRIDGE OPERA HANDBOOKS

General preface

This is a series of studies of individual operas, written for the serious opera-goer or record-collector as well as the student or scholar. Each volume has three main concerns. The first is historical: to describe the genesis of the work, its sources or its relation to literary proto-types, the collaboration between librettist and composer, and the first performance and subsequent stage history. This history is itself a record of changing attitudes towards the work, and an index of general changes of taste. The second is analytical and it is grounded in a very full synopsis which considers the opera as a structure of musical and dramatic effects. In most volumes there is also a musical analysis of a section of the score, showing how the music serves or makes the drama. The analysis, like the history, naturally raises questions of interpretation, and the third concern of each volume is to show how critical writing about an opera, like production and per-formance, can direct or distort appreciation of its structural ele-ments. Some conflict of interpretation is an inevitable part of this account; editors of the handbooks reflect this – by citing classic state-ments, by commissioning new essays, by taking up their own critical position. A final section gives a select bibliography, a discography and guides to other sources.

In working out plans for these volumes, the Cambridge Univer-sity Press was responding to an initial stimulus from staff of the Eng-lish National Opera. Particular thanks are due to Mr Edmund Tracey and Mr Nicholas John for help, advice and suggestions.

Books published
Richard Wagner: *Parsifal* by Lucy Beckett
W. A. Mozart: *Don Giovanni* by Julian Rushton
C. W. von Gluck: *Orfeo* by Patricia Howard
Igor Stravinsky: *The Rake's Progress* by Paul Griffiths
Leoš Janáček: *Kát'a Kabanová* by John Tyrrell
Benjamin Britten: *Peter Grimes* by Philip Brett
Giuseppe Verdi: *Falstaff* by James A. Hepokoski

Other volumes in preparation

For Simonetta Puccini
In affectionate friendship

Contents

Illustrations

1   *Sardou and his 'La Tosca'*

Victorien Sardou (1831–1908) is today scarcely more than a footnote to the history of late nineteenth-century French drama. Were it not for Puccini's opera, based on his play, Sardou's name would probably be known today only to students of French literature. Yet in his time he was a most successful playwright, generally recognized as a born man of the theatre who had all the tricks of his trade at his finger-tips. Modelling his technique on that of his more famous predecessor, Eugène Scribe, who may be said to have initiated what is nowadays called (with some contempt) the 'well-made' play, Sardou wrote a number of stage-works in this genre.[1] An extremely well-thought-out plot, basically naturalistic and which unfolds with almost mathematical logic, stunning *coups de théâtre*, and a dialogue flexible, well-turned and often razor-sharp – these were the positive aspects of Sardou's dramas. Yet there was in them no profundity of thought and feeling, no spiritual, moral or social 'message', no poetry. Sardou's were boulevard dramas in which his supreme aim was to entertain – to entertain as a high-class thriller entertains, creating an atmosphere of mounting suspense and riveting the spectator's attention by means of sensational stage-happenings that were to their author of far greater importance than the exploration of a character's psychology. In a Sardou play, action dwarfs character which is, as it were, only one storey high. 'Sardoodledom' was the unflattering term that G. B. Shaw coined for this kind of play.

Sardou began his career as a satirical writer producing political comedies and comedies of manners in which he pilloried French, in particular Parisian, society of his time. He subsequently turned to serious drama in which the central figure was an historical character or the background an authentic historical event. Thus, in *Théodora* the heroine was the sixth-century Queen of Byzantium; *Madame-Sans-Gêne* dealt with the wife, originally a laundry-girl, of Lefebvre,

1

one of Napoleon's generals; and *La Tosca* is linked with Napoleon's invasion of Italy in 1800 and the fight of the royalists against the republicans. Sardou wrote the majority of his dramas for Sarah Bernhardt – hence his almost invariable choice of a heroine for the central figure – who was one of France's most celebrated actresses, renowned for the extraordinary quality of her voice, which was compared to a 'golden bell', and for her remarkable miming talent. This is the reason for the presence in his plays of long miming scenes, as for instance the scene after Scarpia's murder in *La Tosca*. She was an actress of intense personal projection but, according to Shaw, she never changed, never penetrated a character, but simply overlaid it with her own strong personality. Bernhardt, to whom *La Tosca* is dedicated, went on a number of foreign tours with it; Puccini saw her in Milan in 1890 and again in Florence in October 1895. She did not please him much on this second occasion. He also found the play inferior in poetic situations to Illica's operatic adaptation of it (see below); he was of course judging the play through the eyes of an opera composer. He had only a smattering of French but he was able to follow the action on account of its extraordinary dramatic power and the fact that its situations were self-explanatory; these were his principal criteria whenever he saw a play in a foreign language – French, English, German – and was considering its suitability as an operatic subject.

A man is condemned to death. His wife, mistress or daughter implores the judge or a person of similar authority to pardon him. The judge promises to let the man go on condition that he enjoys her favours for a night. The woman agrees, only to find in the morning that her man has been executed. That is the story of Sardou's play in a nutshell. It appears that this subject had been known since the Middle Ages as potent dramatic material. Shakespeare uses it in *Measure for Measure*; it forms the content of an old Italian ballad said to be still sung in the province of Emilia, and it is the theme of a novel by the nineteenth-century German writer Paul Heyse. In view of this it might seem surprising that, when *La Tosca* was first given in Paris, at the Théâtre de la Porte Saint-Martin on 24 November 1887, accusations of brazen plagiarism should have been raised against Sardou who, to be sure, was never averse to borrowing ideas from other playwrights. Thus Ernest Daudet, brother of the more famous Alphonse, declared that details in Sardou's plot were taken from his own play *La Sainte Aubin*, the heroine of which was a celebrated singer like Tosca, and where the action takes place, as in Sardou, on the eve of Napoleon's battle at Marengo. Like Sardou, Daudet had written the play for Sarah Bernhardt, and the scandal was not without its piquancy, since Daudet asserted that he had read his play to her, implying that the actress had committed an impropriety by giving his plot away to his rival. There was also the American playwright, Maurice Barrymore (founder of the renowned theatrical family), who contended that the theme of Scarpia's infamous bargain with Tosca and his deception of her derived from his play *Nadjezda*. Barrymore succeeded in obtaining an injunction against all American performances of *La Tosca* in English. Sardou, however, energetically denied all these accusations, maintaining that as an avid reader of history he had come across the key-idea for his play in an episode said to have occurred at Toulouse during the religious wars in sixteenth-century France. This episode concerned the Catholic Connétable de Montmorency who promised a Protestant peasant woman that he would save her husband from execution if she gave herself to him. The woman consented but her reward was to see her husband's body dangling from the gallows the next morning.

It is probable that Sardou found a further source for his play in Victor Hugo's drama, *Angélo, tyran de Padoue*, which Arrigo Boito subsequently adapted for the opera *La Gioconda* (1876) by Amilcare Ponchielli, Puccini's composition teacher at the Milan Conservatory. In this opera the title-role is a Venetian street-singer who is pursued by a Scarpia-like character, Barnaba, a spy in the service of the Venetian Inquisition, and who commits suicide rather than yield to Barnaba's desire in exchange for Enzo's life. It is possible that Puccini's first interest in the *Tosca* subject was aroused by Ponchielli's opera. As for the character of Cavaradossi, there is the likelihood that Sardou found his model in the French revolutionary poet André Chénier; both are free-thinkers, both are artists, and both end by being executed. There is, incidentally, an opera *Andrea Chénier* (1896) by Umberto Giordano, containing a scene between Gérard and Maddalena, Chénier's lover, which points directly to the 'Bargain' scene between Scarpia and Tosca in Act II of Puccini's opera. Illica was Giordano's librettist just as he was of the Lucca composer.

However patronizing present-day attitudes towards Sardou may be, it cannot be gainsaid that, on the terms on which he intended *La Tosca* to be taken, it is excellent theatre – melodrama *in excelsis*. In it,

politics, religion, art, love, sex and sadism are inextricably mixed by
the hand of a master-craftsman and geared to a plot of the utmost
ingenuity. Sardou's dramaturgy is impeccable: everything is foreseen
and nothing forgotten, every piece falls into place, there is rhyme and
reason for even the most insignificant detail, and no loose ends are
left hanging – as they are in Puccini. To be sure, Sardou's characters
are scarcely more than puppets – pawns moving on the author's
chessboard according to a master-plan. His mechanics, however,
work too well, the plot unfolds in too clockwork a fashion to achieve
a modicum of credibility and verisimilitude. Indeed, an air of con-
trivance and artificiality hangs over the play, with the result that the
spectator, or rather the reader, remains completely uninvolved in the
fate of Cavaradossi and Tosca. He feels like the public present at a
criminal trial: he is fascinated by the proceedings because of the
fiendishness and enormity of the crime committed by Scarpia on the
two innocent lovers, but he remains a mere observer of the facts, with
his heart untouched. It is only in the opera – and here only to a
limited extent – that, through Puccini's music, Sardou's puppets are
made to breathe, notably through the lyrical episodes, and that the
spectator feels something akin to compassion for Tosca and her
lover.

As I have suggested, *La Tosca* cannot be faulted for its dramaturgy. We may go even farther and say that it shares something with
the drama of character, in that the action springs from traits prominent in both Tosca's and Cavaradossi's personal make-up. In Tosca it
is her insane jealousy, without which Scarpia could not have worked
his clever stratagem, just as Iago could not have worked *his* without
the Moor's fatal disposition. Sardou acknowledges his debt to
Shakespeare when in his Act II (Act I of the opera) he shows Scarpia
being suddenly struck by the idea of using the Marchesa Attavanti's
fan – the lynchpin of his plan – for the same purpose, he says, as Iago
used Desdemona's handkerchief. With Cavaradossi, it is his deep-
seated political conviction as a republican that prompts him to offer
Angelotti his assistance at the risk of his own life and thus makes
him an accomplice of Angelotti's escape in the eyes of Scarpia and
all he stands for. What is most pronounced in both play and opera is
the thriller element: the mounting suspense and tension compounded by Sardou's resort to Grand Guignol – a torture, two attempts at rape, which is tantamount to psychological murder, a real
murder, an execution and two suicides. By the time the last curtain
comes down the body-count is four: Angelotti, Scarpia, Cavaradossi

and Tosca. As Puccini wrote jokingly to his publisher, Giulio Ricordi, after a session with the French playwright: 'Perhaps Sardou will insist on killing Spoletta, too.' Small wonder if after the first performance of *La Tosca* the Parisian critics lambasted it for its scenes of 'butchery and the slaughterhouse'. For its time it was the nonpareil of a *pièce noire*, earning its author the nickname 'Caligula of the stage'.

2 Naturalism in opera: verismo

What was it that caused Puccini to revert in the mid-1890s to the *Tosca* subject, a subject *a tinte forti*, highly coloured which he had rejected some six years earlier? The answer lies in an important change in the operatic climate during the last few decades of the nineteenth-century, a change that followed the turn in European literature from romanticism to realism and its more extreme form, naturalism. This new realist movement, originating in France, was heralded by such writers as Balzac, Flaubert and Dumas *fils*, and culminated in Zola, the foremost practitioner and theoretician of naturalism. In opera the first stirrings were sensed in Verdi's *Luisa Miller* (1849) and notably *La Traviata* (1853), in which for the first time a sexually tainted heroine was brought on to the operatic stage. Naturalism was firmly placed on the operatic map with Bizet's *Carmen* (1875) which became a work of seminal importance for naturalist opera of the following decades. Thus, Alfred Bruneau wrote operas after texts drawn from the novels of Zola, Massenet made a single excursion into naturalism with his two-act *La Navarraise* (1898) and was followed by Charpentier with his *Louise* (1900). In Italy the chief proponents of operatic naturalism or verismo (from *vero* = true) was the group of composers known under the collective name, *giovane scuola italiana* – Mascagni, Leoncavallo, Giordano, and Puccini (*Tosca, Madama Butterfly, La fanciulla del west* and *Il tabarro*). The soil for the *veristi* was well prepared by Italian writers of the time (themselves influenced by the French), such as Luigi Capuana and, notably, Giovanni Verga, who provided the subject for Mascagni's *Cavalleria rusticana* (1890) from one of his short stories of the life of Sicilian peasants and fishermen collected under the title *Vita dei campi*. One of these stories might have almost become an opera by Puccini. While already well into *Bohème*, he toyed with the idea of setting Verga's *La Lupa* – *The She-Wolf* – to music and had begun with the composition; yet he finally gave up the

6

plan because he found Verga's characters 'unattractive, without a single luminous and appealing figure to stand out'. This argues that at that time (1894) he was still averse to pure verismo, but he recycled some of the music for the abortive opera into *Bohème*, for instance Rodolfo's aria 'Nei cieli bigi' (Act I).

Since *Tosca* is a milestone in the relatively short-lived history of verismo, I want to discuss this movement in greater detail. Italian naturalism was certainly not born in the 1890s. A certain tendency to realistic treatment, reflecting a trait in the national character, has been found for centuries in Italian literature – in the episodes of low life in Boccaccio's *Decamerone*, in the *novellieri* of the Renaissance, and lurking in the *commedia dell'arte*. And characters presented in an atmosphere of utter gloom and writhing in paroxysms of passion and suffering have never been portrayed on a more impressive scale than by another great Italian realist – Dante, in his *Inferno*. Nor does it seem to me mere coincidence that Zola, the father of modern literary naturalism, was of Italian origin.

In the late nineteenth century there is a significant difference in the operatic realism of the French and the Italians. With the French there runs a symbolic thread, a kind of universal message through their works. Bruneau's larger theme was the conflict between spiritual and physical forces, a conflict in which, as his mentor Zola declared, the human being suffers and eventually perishes. Again, Charpentier, in his 'musical novel' *Louise*, touched on contemporary problems – free love, the relationship between parents and children, the misery of poverty and the temptation to which *les pauvres* are exposed in a great city like Paris, which is the symbolic heroine of the opera. Italian opera of the time sounds no such ground-bass. Far more earth-bound, yet more vital than their French counterparts, the Italians were almost invariably concerned with the naturalist 'slice of life' in the Here and Now presented in a one-dimensional plot that, save for the eternal and ubiquitous theme of the war between the sexes, scarcely ever allowed a larger, more spiritual theme, let alone poetic symbolism, to intrude.

At the heart of verismo is excess – excess of passion and emotion leading to brutal murder and/or suicide; climax follows climax in quick succession, and no sooner is a mood established than it is destroyed by a contrasting mood. Juxtaposition of scenes of diametrically opposed sentiment is almost a general rule of the *veristi*. After Scarpia's first attempt at rape, Tosca sings a lyrical aria! Characters are presented larger than life, which is one of the inner contradictions of naturalist opera, and are swept along in a white-heat of passion in which sex is the driving force. Erotic desire is thwarted, culminating in acts of murderous jealousy and savage revenge. Such acts – and this is very characteristic – are almost always committed on the open stage so as to score a direct hit on the spectator's sensibilities. Thus, in *Tosca* we are made the witnesses of Cavaradossi's execution, while in Sardou's play it takes place, with classical propriety, off-stage. Again, in Belasco's *The Girl of the Golden West* there is merely talk of lynching Ramarrez; in Puccini's *La fanciulla del west* we actually see the noose placed round his neck.[1] Don José's *crime passionnel* at the end of *Carmen* was the point of departure for all those scenes of stabbing, strangling, execution and suicide on the open stage which we encounter in realist opera of the subsequent period. What encouraged the *veristi* to scenes of extreme passion and violence set in a sombre atmosphere was the fact that they occurred already in what may be called the romantically tinged verismo of Verdi, as in *Ernani, Rigoletto, Trovatore* and *Otello.* In a sense verismo might be defined as the hypertrophic growth of features in the older composer. And we should not forget that the character of the typically Italian operatic voice readily lends itself to the intensification of emotional expression of which French voices are on the whole not capable.

The inner contradictions of the Young Italian School spring from the theory of the verismo movement; some of its tenets were also upheld in practice. Now, realism in the sense of dramatic truth has been known in Italian opera since the time of Monteverdi. Did he not write that the modern composer builds on the foundation of truth? But to build on the foundation of truth and to project truth as it is found in real life are two entirely different things. The first leads to the highest form of realism: imaginative truth; the second to its crudest form: naked realism, which is not the stuff of opera. We recall in this context Verdi's trenchant remark: 'Ah, progress, science, realism! . . . Ahi, ahi! I am a realist as much as you like, but . . . Shakespeare was a realist too, but he did not know it. He was a realist by inspiration, we are realists by design, by calculation.'[2] The stage is to create the illusion of reality, not to photograph it. Moreover, opera is a contrived thing – the most artificial of all the art forms. It has its rules and conventions, which a composer ignores at his peril. Real life has no arias, duets and ensembles. If real life were to be translated faithfully into opera – as was the theoretical aim of the *veristi* – it would at best consist of continuous recitative, with occasional cries and shouts, which would be an impossible proposition. The public at large comes to hear operas with their arias, duets and ensembles and cares less than one might think about dramatic truth.[3] Therein lay the theoretical dilemma of the Italian realists. In practice they composed, like Verdi, 'with one eye on art and with the other on the public'. They did not disdain to write arias, duets and ensembles though, as we shall see, Puccini in *Tosca* avoids, with one exception, real duets; he replaces them with duologues for tenor and soprano alternating with each other and rarely singing together.

I have been dealing so far with the debit side in the ledger of the *veristi*. What of the credit side? Here we must enter such important characteristics as concentration on the essential drama, omission of distracting historical detail, extreme vividness of plot and melodic vigour and vitality, all of which are found in *Tosca*, the opera prophetic of the modern music-theatre. It seems as if these Italian composers were following Zola to the letter when he declared:

Gone is the time when the reader was kept in suspense by a complicated dramatic but improbable story; the sole object is to register human facts, to lay bare the mechanism of body and soul. The plot is simplified; the first man one comes across will do as a hero; examine him and you are sure to find a straightforward drama which allows full play to all the machinery of emotion and passion.[4]

We abstract from this four points which are most relevant to the theory of verismo. The first concerns the rejection of what Zola called a 'complicated dramatic but improbable story'. This means by implication the abandonment of mythical, historical and dynastic subjects and the turning to subjects drawn from ordinary, everyday life – 'the first man one comes across will do as a hero'. From this it follows that almost invariably the heroes and heroines of naturalist opera stand on the lowest rung of the social ladder – hence the gallery of 'low life' characters: prostitutes, soldiers, poor students, workers, peasants and artists. It is perhaps no coincidence that artists figure prominently in several veristic operas – actors in *Pagliacci*, an actress in Cilea's *Adriana Lecouvreur*, a poet in *Andrea Chénier*, a singer and a painter in *Tosca*. Pre-veristic opera already shows this tendency, best seen in Puccini's *La Bohème*, which brings poor artists with their lovers of doubtful virtue on to the stage. There is, thirdly, Zola's demand for 'full play to all the machinery of emotion and passion'; in other words, *le droit divin de la passion* (Zola) forms the central motif in naturalist opera. And, fourthly, there is no better illustration for Zola's 'simplified plot' and 'straightforward drama' than Puccini's libretti, from *Manon Lescaut* to *Turandot*. Verismo also crossed the Alps into Germany, as witness *Das Tiefland* by Eugen d'Albert and *Mona Lisa* by Max von Schillings. And it seems no mere coincidence that Strauss's *Salome* and *Elektra*, which both contain veristic features, were written after *Tosca*. A last echo is heard in *Kátya Kabanova* (1921) by Leoš Janáček, who had already created a Czech brand of Italian realism in *Jenůfa* (1904), and in Shostakovich's *Lady Macbeth of Mtsensk* (1936). And who can deny the verismo element in Alban Berg's *Wozzeck* and *Lulu*?

3   Genesis of 'Tosca'

It was Ferdinando Fontana, the librettist of Puccini's two early operas *Le Villi* (1884) and *Edgar* (1889),[1] who first suggested Sardou's play to Puccini as an operatic subject. This was in early spring 1889, a few months after the first (La Scala) production of *Edgar*. The composer, who acquainted himself with the play through Fontana, was greatly impressed by it, and wrote to his publisher, Giulio Ricordi, on 7 May 1889:

I think of *Tosca*. I beg you to take the necessary steps in order to obtain Sardou's permission. If I had to abandon this idea it would sadden me in the extreme. For I see in this *Tosca* the opera that exactly suits me – an opera without excessive proportions, one not conceived as a decorative spectacle and not requiring the usual superabundance of music.[2]

(Fontana was much piqued when seven years later, after Puccini had decided on *Tosca*, Ricordi called in Giacosa for the versification of the libretto, a task which, as the first to have thought of the French play, he had been hoping for himself and about which he had corresponded with Sardou.)

It seems likely that, because Puccini was at the time a composer without name or mark outside Italy, Sardou at first refused permission for the musicalization of his play. Also, in spite of his evident enthusiasm for the subject Puccini, then sailing in the deep waters of romanticism (*Manon Lescaut*) and later attempting a mixture of romantic and realist elements (*La Bohème*), began to have qualms about a subject of such realistic violence and brutality. Before turning to *Tosca* he produced these two operas, both being of the type known as *tragédie larmoyante*, with characters of a markedly sentimental, soft-grained fibre and demanding a preponderantly lyrical approach. Even when he was well into the composition of *Tosca* he had intermittent spells of doubt as to whether he had after all chosen the right subject, and one suited to his genius. Clear evidence of this is provided by a conversation he once had with Sardou. It began with

11

Puccini saying that it might be better if a French composer were to set the subject to music, to which Sardou replied that it was a Roman subject and so needed an Italian musician. Puccini then cited Verdi and Franchetti, both of whom had considered and finally rejected the subject. Sardou retorted that Verdi's rejection was due not to his being intimidated by the drama, but to his old age – he was too tired to undertake a new opera. Moreover, Sardou continued, the fact that two composers had seriously considered it was the best guarantee of its vitality, and this should encourage Puccini. There followed this dialogue:

Puccini: My music is tenuous, it is delicate, it is written in a different register.
Sardou: There is no register . . . there is only talent.
P.: My previous heroines, Manon and Mimì, are different from Tosca.
S.: Manon, Mimì, Tosca, it's all the same thing!. . . Women in love all belong to the same family. I have created Marcella and Fernanda, I have created Fédora, Théodora and Cléopâtre. They are all the same woman.[3]

Sardou's last remark plainly reveals his limitation as a creator of female characters; which *mutatis mutandis* also applies to the heroines of Puccini's *Manon Lescaut*, *Bohème* and *Butterfly*.

Sardou later claimed that it was largely his powers of persuasion that induced Puccini to write *Tosca*, and he went so far as to admit that the libretto was superior to his play – which in a sense it is. When the opera was first staged in Paris in October 1903, the septuagenarian playwright, exuberant and lively as ever, took full command of the rehearsals, throwing his weight about as if he were not only the author of the play but also composer and producer of the opera as well.

In connexion with the first French production of *Tosca* it seems pertinent to say something a'out Debussy's fierce onslaught on Puccini and the rest of the *giovane scuola italiana*. Debussy's antagonism was dictated partly by his fear of the possible influence this school might have on French music (for he tended to judge all foreign music from an exclusively nationalist, indeed chauvinist, point of view), and partly by his intense dislike of all forms of realism. For this reason he strongly criticized Bruneau, whom he otherwise greatly admired. In an article of 1903 he expressed himself most scathingly about Italian opera of the time:

Inspired by scenes in the realistic cinema the characters throw themselves at one another and appear to wrench melodies from one another's mouths. A whole life is packed into a single act: birth, marriage, and an assassination thrown in. In these one-act operas [*Cavalleria rusticana*, *Pagliacci*] very little music needs to be written, for the reason that there is scarcely any time to hear much.[4]

He thought the worst crime committed by Puccini and Leoncavallo was that they had taken a French novel (Murger's *Scènes de la vie de Bohème*) and made it the theme of operas wholly Italian in spirit; and that, for all their pretence at character study, they achieved nothing more than simple anecdote.[5] (Debussy overlooked the fact that the novel itself is no more than a string of loosely connected episodes or anecdotes in which those dealing with Rodolphe, Marcel, Mimi and Musette happen to be the most important.) To sum up, it appears that Debussy, like most French composers of the time, had no sympathy for Puccini, whose full-blooded realism and emotionalism were poles apart from the ethos of his own music. Puccini, on the other hand, was a fervent admirer of the great French musician in whom he saw the 'soul of an artist capable of the rarest and most subtle perception whose harmonic innovations at first seemed to reveal new forward-looking ideas for musical art'.[6]

We have seen how naturalism invaded Italian opera at the beginning of the 1890s and established verismo. Puccini was unable to resist its strong pull, nor could he, I believe, for reasons of prestige lag behind his Italian fellow-composers. Hence his decision after *Bohème* to write a drama of blood and thunder. But it must be stressed that he was not a verist *pur sang*; he neither began nor ended his career as such. Of his twelve operas only four belong to this genre, of which *Tosca* is perhaps the most characteristic. To be sure, the opera ignores an early tenet of the veristic creed, namely to show a *contemporary* 'slice of life' and, like Giordano's *Andrea Chénier* of four years earlier, deals with a story set in the historical past. Nor could its extraordinary happenings be called a 'slice of life'. But in spirit and treatment it wholly conforms to the principles of verismo.

   In addition one must consider two aspects of Puccini's own psychological make-up. One was his inherent sadism, his 'neronic instincts' as he put it, which may be defined in his own words as 'grande dolore in piccole anime' – 'Great sorrow in little souls'; this was an *Ur*-motif in his operatic thinking, the grit in his oyster as it were. The second was his largely unconscious equation of erotic love with sin or guilt, to be atoned for by death or suicide; it runs through every one of his tragic operas. This is borne out by careful study of his psychology as reflected in his letters and, notably, his libretti.[7] The lovers and their fate in *Tosca* are a prime illustration of this.

Two adventitious but not unimportant events confirmed Puccini in his belief that in *Tosca* he had, for all his intermittent doubts, chosen the right subject. The first was the fact that his rival Alberto Franchetti (*Asrael, Cristoforo Colombo, Germania*), had signed a contract with Ricordi for an opera based on Sardou's *La Tosca* for which Luigi Illica had written the libretto. In the autumn of 1894 Franchetti and Illica travelled to Paris to discuss with Sardou the operatic adaptation of his drama. It so happened that at a session during which Illica read his libretto to a small gathering, the old Verdi was also present. He was a friend of Sardou's, and his attendance in Paris was required for the first French production of his *Otello*. Verdi is said to have been so deeply impressed by this reading, notably by a long 'Farewell to Art and Life' (not in Sardou or Puccini) to be sung by Cavaradossi shortly before his execution, that he snatched the manuscript from Illica's hand and read the verses aloud in a trembling voice. Verdi later said that he would himself have wanted to set *La Tosca* to music provided that Sardou had allowed him to change the ending of the opera, but he was now too old for this.[8]

Verdi's reaction at this reading was promptly reported to Puccini, and this, combined with his knowledge that Franchetti planned to write a *Tosca*, served to put a singularly high premium on this subject. He determined to have it, by hook or by crook. Ricordi, who knew only too well which of the two composers would make a better job of it, resorted to a stratagem that in present-day terms might be called 'psychological warfare'. With Puccini's knowledge and consent, the publisher and his 'accomplice' Illica set about dissuading Franchetti from setting *Tosca*. They said that after long consideration they had come to the conclusion that it was a most unsuitable subject for an opera. They spoke of the coarse brutality of the plot, pointing in particular to Scarpia's attempted rape of the heroine as a scene far too *risqué* for the Italian public, especially since it was followed by Scarpia's murder at Tosca's hand; this, they said, was bound to alienate the public's sympathy for the heroine. They clinched their argument by referring to historical details of the play which would be incomprehensible to a modern audience. The ruse worked. Franchetti's confidence in the subject was demolished and he proceeded to renounce his composing right. This happened in the autumn of 1895 when Puccini had already made up his mind to write a *Tosca*. (It is not known what Franchetti's reaction was when he heard that Puccini was using the same subject.) From the ethical point of view Ricordi's conduct was disgraceful, but thanks to it, the world of opera has been enriched by one of the most powerful musical stage-works in the repertory.

If Puccini needed further confirmation that he had chosen an excellent subject, it came in a letter from Ricordi of 14 October 1896 in which the publisher told him that he and Illica had paid Verdi a three-hour visit in which the old composer was brought up to date about 'what new works were on the stocks'. When told about Puccini's *Tosca* he exclaimed: 'Puccini has a good libretto! Fortunate the composer who has that work in hand!' 'Our Verdi', Ricordi concluded, 'is a good prophet!! Therefore *laboremus*!!'[9]

The two librettists Illica and Giacosa had been Puccini's collaborators in *Bohème* and were to be again in *Madama Butterfly*. It is of some interest that Puccini was one of the first Italian composers to have two writers working in tandem for him – a practice that originated in nineteenth-century France, in both drama and opera: for instance, Scribe's collaboration with Legouvé in *Adrienne Lecouvreur* and Meilhac's with Halévy in *Carmen* and some Offenbach operettas. Illica and Giacosa had first collaborated as two of the five anonymous authors of the libretto of *Manon Lescaut*.

Luigi Illica (1857–1919) counts for little in Italian literature and drama; his occasional ventures into poetic verse were mockingly nicknamed 'Illicasilibi'. But he made his mark as one of the most sought-after librettists of the time, with some 30-odd opera books to his name. He was quick-witted, resourceful and a swift worker, excelling in the invention of telling theatrical incidents and the elaboration of a given subject into an interesting plot. His eye for the operatic stage was even keener than Puccini's, which is saying a great deal, and he had more practical sense of what was possible in the theatre than Giacosa and the composer. Illica was never at a loss for an idea and, often on the spur of the moment, would light on an effective way out of a scenic or dramatic impasse that had baffled the other two men.

Giuseppe Giacosa (1847–1906) on the other hand belonged to the front rank of those Italian writers and playwrights whose works formed the transition from the romanticism of Carducci and Pascoli to the French-inspired naturalism of the last two decades of the nineteenth century. Giacosa was a gifted poet and essayist and the author of finely observed short stories. But, above all, he was a dramatist with a subtle psychological insight, with a considerable number of tragedies and comedies to his name, of which *Tristi amori* (1887) and *La Dame de Challent* (1891) – the first written for Eleonora Duse and the second for Sarah Bernhardt – won him international acclaim. Giacosa was also the editor of the prestigious literary periodical *La Lettura*. The employment of so eminent a writer as a librettist argues the growing importance that was being attached to the literary quality of an operatic text, a tendency undoubtedly inspired by Verdi's collaboration with Boito and which seems ultimately to have originated with Wagner's own libretti.

There was a clear division of labour between Illica and Giacosa. While Illica drew up the scenario and developed the plot in detail, Giacosa saw to the versification of the prose-text, elaborated Puccini's lyrical situations, introduced a more balanced distribution of the scenes, and generally gave the libretto a more refined literary polish. Although there were many quarrels and confrontations between the two and between them and Puccini (a hard taskmaster), requiring the diplomatic intervention of Giulio Ricordi, Illica and Giacosa complemented each other in an almost ideal way. Puccini was never again to have such a team of collaborators and it is no coincidence that the libretti of his three most successful operas were fashioned by Illica and Giacosa.

Compared with the labour and toil spent on the libretti of *Manon Lescaut* and *Bohème*, which were both drawn from once celebrated novels, the adaptation of the *Tosca* text went relatively smoothly since its source was a play, although it needed both condensation and expansion in order to make it suitable to Puccini's purposes. (It should be added that, of Puccini's subsequent operas, four were based on plays which had had considerable success in their time: (*Butterfly*, *La fanciulla del west*, *Il tabarro* and *Turandot*.)

From a letter of Giacosa to Ricordi[10] dated 23 August 1896, we gather that the skilful adaptation of the French play and the transposition of scenes were the work of Illica who, we recall, had already prepared a version for Franchetti which was, most probably, the basis for the Puccini text. The difficulties which arose were very largely caused by Giacosa's intense dislike of Sardou's drama. At first glance, he writes in his letter, it appears suitable for operatic treatment because of the rapidity with which its action unfolds and because of its self-explanatory situations. Yet the more he studies each scene and tries to extract poetic and lyrical moments from them, the more convinced he becomes of its absolute unadaptability for the musical stage. For Giacosa *Tosca* was a coarse emotional drama in which incident prevailed over poetry. In an earlier letter he had claimed that while *Bohème* was all poetry with barely a plot, *Tosca* was all plot with no poetry.[11] Moreover, he reminds Ricordi that even in the spoken theatre *La Tosca* had never become part of the normal repertory, being essentially a display-piece for an exceptional actress.[12] (The Parisian revival of Sardou's play in 1909 seems to have been largely due to the popularity which Puccini's opera had achieved in the meantime.) In another letter (14 December 1896)[13] Giacosa criticizes the dramatic treatment of Scarpia saying, with reference to his monologue at the opening of Act II ('Ha più forte sapore'), that a character such as Scarpia does not express himself in words but in acts. he thought the monologue a dramatic and psychological absurdity, but admitted that as a non-musician he was not in a position to judge its necessity in the opera. He was also sarcastic about the psychology of Cavaradossi, the '*signor tenore*, as you call him (for it seems that for you and Puccini Cavaradossi should be nothing but a *signor tenore*) . . . You wanted lyrical verses and we know that lyrical verses have nothing to do with psychology or dramaturgy. So let it be lyrical verses!'[14] Giacosa clearly despised the *Tosca* libretto and worked at it with great reluctance. After one of his several *contretemps* with Puccini and Ricordi, he offered to resign.

By the end of October 1896 Puccini was in possession of the greater part of the libretto (Acts I and II) and was looking forward to receiving the final act. Composition started, in a desultory fashion, and did not get going seriously until spring 1898, according to Puccini's entry in the autograph score. Work on the opera had to be interrupted several times, since the composer was invited to supervise foreign productions of *Manon Lescaut* and *Bohème*. On the occasion of the first French production of *Bohème* (Paris, May 1896) Puccini had, on Ricordi's advice, paid his first visit to Sardou in order to discuss points in the *Tosca* libretto in which the playwright wished to take an active hand.[15] Of the meeting Puccini later gave his first biographer, Arnaldo Fraccaroli, this lively account:[16]

The man was prodigious. He was then more than seventy [actually sixty-five] but there was in him the energy and agility of a youngster. Besides, he was an indefatigable and highly interesting conversationalist, talking for hours on end without getting tired. When he touched on an historical subject, he was a water-tap, nay, a fountain; anecdote after anecdote would pour from his lips in a clear and inexhaustible stream. Our session simply turned into monologues – most delightful of course, but this did not make for much progress with our *Tosca*. However, he suddenly became compliant and readily accepted the need to suppress one act [Act II of the play] and to fuse the scene in the prison cell with that of the execution [Act V scenes 1 and 2 of the play].

Puccini began composition by starting with the Act I finale – Scarpia's monologue and the *Te Deum*. Although well acquainted with the liturgy from his early days as organist at the Cathedral of San Martino in Lucca, he was anxious to achieve strict fidelity, and wished to make absolutely certain of the prayer that is customarily recited in Roman churches during the Cardinal's procession from the sacristy to the High Altar, whenever a solemn *Te Deum* is sung. He first thought of the *Ecce Sacerdos* but feeling that this was not quite suitable for his purpose, it occurred to him that an old Latin sequence would do. After abortive attempts to find such verses he remembered a priest of his acquaintance, Father Pietro Panichelli,[17] to whom he wrote in August 1898. He made an explicit request for the words of a prayer which, for the phonic effect he had in mind, had to be 'murmured in subdued and muttered voices, without intonation, precisely as real prayers are said'.

The *Ecce Sacerdos* [Puccini continued] is too imposing to be murmured. I know that it is not usual to say or sing anything before the solemn *Te Deum* which is sung as soon as they reach the High Altar, but I repeat (whether rightly or wrongly) that I should like to find *something to be murmured* during the procession from the sacristy to the altar, either by the Chapter or the people; preferably by the people because they are more numerous and therefore more effective musically.[18]

Panichelli was unable to find a suitable text, and Puccini eventually rooted one out in an old Latin prayer book. The repetition of the vowels 'o' and 'u' produces the dull, dark sound the composer intended:

> Adjutorum nostrum in nomine Domini
> Qui fecit coelum et terram
> Sit nomen Domini benedictum
> Et hoc nunc et usque seculum.

But Father Panichelli gave Puccini the version of the plainsong in which the *Te Deum* is sung in the churches of Rome, since a number of variant forms are used in the different dioceses of Italy. He also gave the composer a detailed description of the correct order of the Cardinal's procession to the High Altar and of the costumes worn by the Swiss Guard, and put him in touch with old Maestro Meluzzi of St Peter's, a specialist in campanology, as Puccini wanted to reproduce in Act III the authentic effect of the Matin bells, the *scampanio*

mattutino, which are rung from various Roman churches to announce the first *Ave Maria*; in particular he wished to know the exact
pitch of St Peter's largest bell, the famous *campanone*; Meluzzi
established this – not without difficulty, because of its powerful over-
tones – as the E below the bass stave, which is duly sounded by the
lowest bell in Act III of the opera. In addition, Puccini went specially
to Rome, and early one morning climbed up to the rampart of the
Castel Sant'Angelo in order to obtain a first-hand impression of the
Matin bells rung from the churches all around the fortress. This is
an illustration of Puccini's predilection for what one might call
'documentary' realism – that is, the reproduction of authentic detail
from real life, a predilection manifest in all his mature operas and
one which he shared with writers such as Zola and Flaubert. Zola,
for example, spent months in the coal-mines of northern France and
in the slums of Paris in order to create the right ambiance in his
novels *Germinal* and *L'Assommoir*; Flaubert carefully noted the
clinical details of arsenic poisoning for *Madame Bovary*; and this is
on a par with Puccini's researches.

In his search for authenticity, characteristic of the *veristi*, the
composer also approached Luigi Zanazzo, a Roman poet and librar-
ian at the Ministry of Education, from whom he obtained the verses
for the little pastoral, 'Io de' sospiri', sung by the shepherd in Act III.
The pair of quatrains is in the style of the traditional shepherd songs
of the Roman Campagna, and Puccini particularly wanted it not to
refer in any way to the actual drama of *Tosca*. He sent the poet
dummy verses in order to show him the kind of metre he required,
which suggests, as do other instances in Puccini's operas, that he had
already sketched the music before he had the words for it.

One of the many quarrels between composer and librettists concerned the 'torture' scene (Act II) where Illica had originally written
words for a funereal aria for Cavaradossi, to be sung *during* his torture and then debouching into a quartet with Tosca, Spoletta and the
Judge. Puccini found this formal piece unacceptable, since it went
against all dramatic verisimilitude and represented a reversion to
obsolete conventions. Another quarrel, lasting until the opera was all
but finished (September 1899), was over Cavaradossi's famous
'Farewell to Art and Life' which had moved the old Verdi so profoundly at that session at Sardou's. Illica had written it in a reflective,
somewhat philosophical vein with verses of a rhetorical cast, but
Puccini wanted a stirring *lamento* – the present 'E lucevan le stelle' –
expressing a lover's agony at having to leave his beloved for ever, the

conjunction of Eros and Thanatos being one of the mainsprings of the composer's dramatic art. Illica, proud of his verses and recalling Verdi's reaction to them, was at first adamant in his refusal to change them, ignoring the fact that the rhetorical and philosophical mode was entirely alien to Puccini's creative thinking. Matters were complicated by the composer having already sketched music to his own words for Cavaradossi's aria, words that precisely characterized the hero's desperate mood at this point of the drama.[19] The arguments over the change were long-drawn-out, and were not settled until Puccini brought Illica round to his point of view, by singing the music of his lament to his librettists accompanying himself on the piano. Giacosa was entrusted with writing new verses, adapting their metre to the composer's melody and retaining from his text the two words, 'Muoio disperato!'[20] Puccini later jokingly declared that admirers of 'E lucevan le stelle' had triple cause to be grateful to him: for composing the music, for causing the new words to be written, and for declining expert advice to throw the result into the waste-paper basket.[21]

In this context two effective changes in the text must be mentioned, both occurring in Act II and both made by Puccini. The librettists, following the French original, made Scarpia ask Tosca, 'Tu mi odii?' – 'You hate me?' The composer turned this question into the far more telling, 'Come tu mi odii!' – 'How you hate me!' His second contribution was in Tosca's famous phrase 'E avanti a lui tremava tutta Roma!' – 'And before him used to tremble all Rome!', spoken tonelessly as she quietly contemplates Scarpia lying dead on the floor. The line in Sardou reads, 'Et c'est devant ça que tremblait toute une ville'. – 'And before that trembled a whole city'. 'Ça' expresses Tosca's utter contempt for this 'thing' lying dead at her feet; she cannot believe that a 'whole city' trembled before it. Puccini's 'tutta Roma' conjures up the terror of Scarpia's reign: before him there trembled not just a vague 'whole city' but the Eternal City itself. For some reason the librettists had taken out this phrase.[22] Minimal though these changes may seem, they result in a subtle shift of meaning and evidently belong to what Verdi called 'la parola scenica' – 'the scenic word': by which he meant a verbal phrase so turned as to sum up a situation or a character's feeling in the most concise form. Tosca's phrase is an excellent example of this, and so is her parting shot before she flings herself to her death: 'O Scarpia, avanti a Dio!'.

A last hitch occurred when the opera was already finished.[23] This time it was Ricordi who, after reading the final act, objected to the love duet of Tosca and Cavaradossi. Writing to Puccini on 10 October 1899, he said:

> It is fragmentary music, music of meagre line that reduces the characters to pygmies . . . I find that one of the most beautiful passages of lyrical poetry – 'O dolci mani!' – is merely underlaid by a scrappy and modest little melody which, to make matters worse, comes from *Edgar*! Stupendous if sung by a peasant woman from the Tyrol, but out of place in the mouth of Tosca and Cavaradossi.[24]

On all previous occasions Ricordi's criticism had carried weight with Puccini, but this time, convinced that what he had written was right, he stuck to his guns, as becomes clear from his letter of 11 October, a day after the receipt of Ricordi's outburst:

> You know how scrupulous I am in interpreting situations and words, and how important this is before putting anything down on paper. Your reproach about having taken a fragment from *Edgar* – this may be criticized by you and those few who are capable of recognizing it, and it can be regarded as a labour-saving [*schivafatica*] device. As it stands (if one discards the notion that it comes from another work – Act IV of *Edgar* abolished anyhow) it seems full of the poetry which breathes out of the words . . . As for its fragmentary character, that was deliberate. This love duet cannot be a steady and tranquil situation as is the case with other love duets. In thought Tosca is constantly returning to the need for Mario's fall to be well simulated and for his behaviour to appear natural in front of the firing squad.[25]

So far as we know, Puccini altered not a note in this duet. Incidentally, Ricordi was mistaken in saying that Puccini's self-borrowing occurred in 'O dolci mani!'; the actual passage taken over from Act IV of *Edgar* is in the middle section of the love duet, in the *Andante amoroso* beginning with 'Amaro sol per te'; the key and orchestration are identical with those of the *Edgar* passage, but the melody has been radically modified.

4 Synopsis

Act I

(The church of Sant'Andrea della Valle. At the right, the Attavanti Chapel. On the left, a scaffolding, on which stands a large picture on an easel covered by a piece of cloth. Painter's tools lie about, also a basket.)

The opera has no formal overture but opens abruptly with the motto-like 'Scarpia' motif (Ex. la) (*fff tutta forza*) that expresses the

Ex. 1a 'Scarpia' motto

Ex. 1b 'Well' motif

Ex. 1c 'Reflection' motif

22

essential atmosphere of the drama[1] – the cruelty, violence and brutality personified in the central character. Angelotti, a political prisoner, who has escaped from the fortress of Castel Sant' Angelo, enters the church from a side entrance. Dishevelled, trembling with fear and out of breath, he casts a quick look round. His state of mind is reflected in two musical ideas – a syncopated figure in a descending fourth (*ff, Vivacissimo con violenza*) (Ex. 2a) and a chain of chromatically slithering tritones or augmented fourths *p* (woodwind) (Ex. 2b) to which is later added a cantabile motif (*dolce*) as he notices the pillar-shrine with an image of the Madonna (violins). He approaches it, for his sister, the Marchesa Attavanti, has written to him saying that she has hidden the key to the Attavanti chapel at the foot of the pillar. He cannot at first find the key, and frantically searches until, with a smothered cry of joy, he finds it. Gripped by renewed fear that he may be observed, he carefully inserts the key into the lock, opens the gate, relocks it from inside and hides in the chapel. The scene is clinched by the reappearance of Exx. 2a and 2b.

Ex. 2a 'Angelotti' motif (1)

Ex. 2b 'Angelotti' motif (2)

Ex. 2c Angelotti's 'Escape' motif

Ex. 3 'Sacristan' motif

The Sacristan arrives, thinking the noise he has heard was caused by Cavaradossi. He is characterized by a scherzo-like *ballabile* theme (*Allegretto grazioso*), its skipping fourths and the staccato suggesting his unconscious comicality (Ex. 3). He looks up at the scaffolding and is surprised to find no one there. Climbing up, he looks into the food-basket and finds it untouched. As he climbs down again the Angelus is rung. He kneels and quietly intones the prayer 'Angelus Domini . . .' (*Andante religioso*). Cavaradossi enters, and seeing the Sacristan kneeling asks him what he is doing. Cavaradossi's question is designed to show his ignorance of religious customs and by implication his atheism. He mounts the scaffold to the broad 'Cavaradossi' theme (Ex. 4a) (woodwind and horns) and uncovers the painting, which shows a Mary Magdalene with large blue eyes and golden hair, the orchestra throwing out a hint at the later 'Love' theme, Ex. 4e. Seeing the painting, the Sacristan furiously exclaims 'Sante ampolle! Il suo ritratto! – 'By all the saints, it is her portrait!' He is referring to the unknown lady (Attavanti) who, he says, has been coming these last few days to pray so devoutly before the Madonna. Cavaradossi says that she has been so absorbed in prayer that, unseen by her, he has painted her lovely features. 'Fuori, Satana, fuori!' – 'Away, Satan, away!' is the Sacristan's enraged reaction. Cavaradossi begins to paint, while the Sacristan comes and goes, picking up the brushes and washing them in a basin. Suddenly Cavaradossi stops painting, takes from his pocket a medallion containing a miniature of Tosca and lets his eyes move between the miniature and the painting. He compares the two women – Tosca with her black eyes and Mary Magdalene with her blue ones – and is moved to ponder the mysterious harmony of art that may bring together such contrasting beauties (aria, 'Recondita armonia') (see p. 102).

Ex. 4a 'Cavaradossi' theme

Ex. 4b Tosca's 'entrance' theme

Ex. 4c Tosca's arietta 'Non la sospiri'

Ex. 4d Cavaradossi's 'Love' motif: arietta 'Qual occhio al mondo'

Ex. 4e 'Love' motif

Ex. 4f Finale of Act I (Ecclesiastical theme)

Ex. 4g Scarpia's aria 'Ha più forte sapore'

Ex. 4h Scarpia's monologue 'Già mi struggea l'amor'

Ex. 4i 'Torture' motif

Ex. 4j From the prelude to Act III

Ex. 4k 'Trionfal di nuova speme'

The Sacristan angrily comments that these different women compete with the Madonna and give off a stench of hell-fire; but it is no good arguing with these Voltairean dogs (such as Cavaradossi) – they are enemies of the Holy Church. These remarks denote the antagonism between the Sacristan and the painter – the religious bigot and royalist and the free-thinker and republican. Before leaving, the Sacristan points to the food-basket, but Cavaradossi says he is not hungry. The cleric cannot suppress a joyful gesture and with a greedy glance places the basket to one side. Taking two pinches from his snuff box he tells the painter to shut the church before departing, and happily shuffles off, to his theme (Ex. 3).

While Cavaradossi continues painting, Angelotti, believing the church to be empty, now opens the gate of the chapel. With his appearance the mood of the previous scene changes to one of high agitation announced by the re-entry of his motif (Ex. 2a). The noise at first causes Cavaradossi to wonder whether there are people in the church. Angelotti stops, terrified, thinking he should hide again in the chapel, but as he raises his eyes he gives a cry of joy, for he recognizes the painter and stretches his arm out to him as though to a saviour. This is accompanied in the orchestra by a new theme, *ff marcatissimo*, chromatically rising and falling within the interval of a fourth and possibly expressing Angelotti's excitement at the unexpected meeting with an old acquaintance. The painter at first fails to recognize him. 'Has prison changed me so much?' Angelotti asks. After a moment's hesitation, Cavaradossi exclaims, 'Angelotti! The Consul of the ill-fated Roman Republic!' and at once offers him his help – 'disponete di me!' – 'You can count on me!' All this is said rapidly and with force, unaccompanied, so that every word is clearly heard. As Angelotti tells the painter about his escape from the Castel Sant'Angelo, we hear an important new theme, a somewhat fragmented idea (Ex. 2c), into which cuts the first of Tosca's calls offstage, 'Mario!', based on the opening of the 'Love' theme (Ex. 4e) (flute, *p*). The painter says that Tosca is an extremely suspicious and jealous woman, but she will not stay long, and he urges Angelotti to hide in the chapel. Seeing that he is nearly fainting with hunger, he gives him his food-basket. Tosca repeats her call four more times, the last three times angrily in close succession, before Cavaradossi, pretending the utmost calm, opens the church-door to her.

(Beginning of the love scene) Tosca enters, the orchestra announcing her beautifully shaped lyrical theme (Ex. 4b), but violently refuses Cavaradossi's attempt to embrace her. Looking suspiciously around, she bombards him with jealous questions: 'Why was the church-door closed? Who were you speaking to? You were whispering something. Where is she? That woman![2] I heard steps and the rustle of skirts.' Cavaradossi's reply is that she must be dreaming. Denying everything, he says he loves only her. He tries to kiss her but she gently reproves him – 'What? In front of the Madonna?' She goes to the statue of the Holy Virgin, arranging the flowers she has brought with her, then kneels in prayer, crosses herself and rises: all this designed to display her intense piety. Cavaradossi has meanwhile continued painting. This dialogue unfolds against Tosca's 'Entrance' (Ex. 4b) which Puccini expands into a broad lyrical melody of eight bars.[3]

Tosca explains that she has come to tell Cavaradossi she will be singing this evening at the opera, but since the piece is short he is to await her at the stage-door, and then they will go to his villa in the country to spend the night there. He listens, but his thoughts are elsewhere: the syncopated 'Angelotti' motif (Ex. 2a), suddenly cutting in, tells us where. It will be full moon tonight, Tosca remarks, and the scent of flowers will be ravishing, these romantic phrases being set to an expressive arioso in G sharp minor. 'Will that please you?' she asks, and Cavaradossi coolly replies 'Very much'. Struck by his tone, she tries to arouse his ardour by describing their love nest (arietta, 'Non la sospiri la nostra casetta' (Ex. 4c), in which a graceful cadential figure (Ex. 5a) makes a repeated appearance, as it will later when

Ex. 5a Cadential figure

Ex. 5b

l'in - na - mo - ra - ta   To - sca è pri - gio - nie - ra____

1   Act I. Maria Callas as Tosca and Renato Cioni as Cavaradossi, Covent Garden, 1964

Ex. 6 'Attavanti' theme

e te, bel-ta - de i - gno - ta,_____ cin- ta di chio-me bion - de

Cavaradossi urges Angelotti to hide in the villa outside Rome. The figure seems to be closely associated with the idea of the villa). Cavaradossi succumbs to her romantic mood, but soon pretends that he must return to his work – 'Urge l'opera, lo sai' ('the work demands it, you know'), he says meaningfully ('Angelotti' motif, Ex. 2a). Tosca is about to depart when her glance falls on the painting. In great agitation she asks, 'Who is that fair-haired woman there?' 'The Madonna', answers Cavaradossi, 'You like her?' 'She is too beautiful', Tosca replies. But she has seen those blue eyes before. 'Wait! It is the Attavanti!',[4] she exclaims; and overcome by her insane jealousy she demands to know, 'La vedi? T'ama? Tu l'ami?' – 'You see her? She loves you? You love her?' The footsteps and that whispering she heard must have been those of the Attavanti. Cavaradossi replies that it was pure chance that he painted her, unnoticed by her. Tosca makes him swear that this is the truth but she is still troubled by the blue eyes of the painting. He assures here that no eyes in the world could compare with her own lustrous black eyes (arietta, 'Qual' occhio al mondo' (Ex. 4d)). Tosca calms down but still wants the eyes painted black! The love duet proper begins ('Mia gelosa' (Ex. 4e)) which represents the lyrical climax of the first act. It ends with the lovers' kiss, Cavaradossi gently reproving Tosca with the words she uttered at the opening of the love scene – 'What? Kissing in front of the Madonna?' 'She is so good', replies Tosca and leaves, but not before firing a parting shot with her coquettish 'But paint her eyes black!' (The whole scene, beginning with Tosca's entrance, is discussed on p. 104).

No sooner has she departed than Cavaradossi rushes to the gate of the Attavanti chapel, opens it and warmly shakes hands with Angelotti who has of course overheard the whole conversation. The painter explains that Tosca hides nothing from her father confessor and that was why he kept silent about Angelotti. When the latter mentions his sister, the painter realizes that the unknown lady whom he had suspected of coming to the church for a secret tryst was the Attavanti; ostensibly she came for fervent prayer, but in reality to hide under the altar a veil, a fan and women's clothing with which

2   Act II. Gabriel Bacquier (left) as Scarpia, Metropolitan Opera House, 1968/9

Angelotti is to disguise himself when making his escape from the church. At his mention of Scarpia's name (it is at this point that we hear Ex. 1a for the first time within the actual opera) Cavaradossi utters a curse: 'bigot and satyr', 'that confessor and executioner!'; he will save Angelotti even at the cost of his own life. Angelotti's plan is to wait for escape until the evening, but the painter feels that delay would be unsafe and tells him to make his way to his villa; if danger threatens he is to hide in the well of the garden. At this point is heard the 'Well' motif (Ex. 1b) which, with its whole-tone bass, is a derivative of the 'Scarpia' motif (Ex. 1a); there is musical logic in this derivation, since it is in the well that Angelotti, pursued by Scarpia's henchmen, will commit suicide (Act II).

Cavaradossi has hardly finished speaking when a cannon shot is heard from the Castel Sant'Angelo, showing that Angelotti's escape has been discovered. He bids the painter a hasty farewell, but Cavaradossi now decides to go with him and the two depart hurriedly. The Sacristan rushes in (Ex. 3), breathless with excitement, wanting to tell Cavaradossi the great news that Napoleon has been beaten by the Austrians – news that is bound to upset the painter – but he is surprised to find nobody in the church. He is soon surrounded by a noisy crowd of choristers and he tells them of the defeat of Napoleon who was 'spennato, sfracellato e piombato a Belzebù!' – 'plucked, smashed and sent to the devil!' The choristers first laugh this off with 'E sogno, è fola' – 'It's a dream, a fairy-tale' – but he assures them that the news has just come in and that a great celebration will take place in the Palazzo Farnese, and Floria Tosca is to sing in a special cantata. The choristers do not take much notice of what he says – they are excited at the prospect of receiving double pay for singing in a festival *Te Deum* in the church. They continue laughing and shouting as he vainly tries to hustle them into the sacristy to change for the ceremony. All this takes place in a spirited *Allegro* in 6/8 and 9/8 time, with the skip of a fourth upwards suggesting their excitement.

At the height of the pandemonium Scarpia suddenly appears at the door with Spoletta and his other henchmen; Ex. 1a interrupts and the choristers stop abruptly in the middle of a word ('vitto-'), as though an evil spell had been cast upon them. Scarpia orders them to get ready for the *Te Deum* but commands the Sacristan to stay for an interrogation; Ex. 7 combines the 'Scarpia' motif with that of the Sacristan. A prisoner, says Scarpia, has escaped from the Castel Sant'Angelo, is believed to have taken refuge in the church and may

Ex. 7

still be here. 'Where is the chapel of the Attavanti?' he asks the Sacristan. The latter goes to the chapel and is nonplussed at finding another key in the lock. Scarpia, considering this valuable evidence, enters the chapel himself but comes out annoyed at having found nothing there, except a fan. 'That cannon-shot was a great mistake', he reflects, for it gave Angelotti time to escape, but he has left a precious piece of evidence behind – the fan, which suggests that he must have had a female accomplice. Examining the fan carefully, he notices the coat of arms of the Attavanti family on it, and glancing at the painting of Mary Magdalene he recognizes the features of the Marchesa. 'Who painted this?', he asks the Sacristan. 'Il cavaliere Cavaradossi!' (Ex. 4a). 'He! Tosca's lover!', Scarpia exclaims, 'A man under suspicion! A Voltairean!' Meanwhile one of his agents has come out of the chapel with Cavaradossi's empty food-basket. The Sacristan is surprised at this, as he had left the basket full of delicacies on the scaffolding. 'He may have eaten it', says Scarpia. But this is impossible, retorts the cleric, for the chapel was closed and Cavaradossi had no key. Besides, did he not say that he was not hungry? It now becomes clear to the Chief of Police that it is Angelotti who has eaten the food that the greedy Sacristan had put to one side for himself.

The Sacristan's interrogation unfolds in a recitative accompanied in the orchestra by such relevant motifs and themes as Angelotti's 'Escape' (Ex. 2c), the 'Attavanti' figure (Ex. 6), 'Cavaradossi' theme (Ex. 4a), the Sacristan's theme (Ex. 3), which is about the only one to undergo motivic variations, and the 'Angelotti' motif (Ex. 2a).

Tosca suddenly arrives, to the 'Love' theme (Ex. 4e). She has come back in order to tell Cavaradossi that they cannot meet this evening as arranged, since she has to sing in the cantata at the Palazzo Farnese to celebrate the Austrians' (supposed) victory over the French. She is very much on edge, as she cannot find her lover who, the Sacristan remarks, has vanished into thin air as if by witchcraft.

Scarpia has hidden himself behind a pillar and is scheming how to make use for his own purposes of Tosca's great weakness – her insane jealousy; 'Iago had a handkerchief', he says to himself, 'I have a fan!' He comes forward startling Tosca with his sudden appearance. Dipping his fingers into the stoup, he offers her holy water. She touches his fingers slightly and crosses herself. With simulated gallantry he flatters Tosca, saying that she has set a noble example by coming to the church to pray – unlike other women who come here secretly to meet their lovers. At the same time he points meaningfully to the painting. This exchange is set to an *Andante mosso* in E flat major which is based on an ostinato-like bell motif of four notes (B flat– G–A flat–F); together with its subsequent melodic expansion it well suggests the wheedling, honeyed manner of Scarpia. Tosca has understood, but angrily demands concrete proof of his insinuation. He shows her the fan, on which she recognizes the coat of arms of the Attavanti. Her jealousy is now fully roused, confirming her suspicion of Cavaradossi's infidelity, and in a sad arioso ('Ed io venivo a lui', the climax of which is the phrase 'l'innamorata Tosca è prigioniera' (Ex. 5b)) she laments the fact that she has to sing for the Queen this evening. In her mind she sees her lover in the arms of the Marchesa at the villa, now besmirched with mud; she will surprise them in their love nest. Scarpia, who has been watching her, makes melodramatic asides: 'Ho sortito l'effetto!. . . Già il veleno l'ha rosa! . . . Morde il veleno' ('I have achieved the desired effect. . . Already the poison is working. . . the poison begins to bite'). Hypocritically he offers Tosca consoling words saying that he would give his life to wipe the tears from her cheeks. With sudden resolution Tosca turns to the painting: 'You shall not have him!' This last dialogue is dominated by two of the 'Angelotti' motifs (Ex. 2a and c). To the accompaniment of the 'Love' theme (Ex. 4e) Scarpia escorts Tosca to the door, while the church fills with people who have come to pray and await the Cardinal's arrival. No sooner has Tosca departed than Scarpia summons Spoletta, ordering him to take three agents and a carriage, to follow her wherever she goes, and report to him later at the Palazzo Farnese. The Cardinal enters with his escort and walks towards the High Altar, the music now taking on an ecclesiastical character in a *Largo religioso* (Finale I, see p. 108) which is based on Example 4f and during which Scarpia has his monologue, 'Va Tosca! Nel tuo chor s'annida Scarpia!' – 'Go, Tosca! In your heart lodges Scarpia!' As the Cardinal passes him he kneels, but his thoughts are with Cavaradossi and Tosca – 'The one to the gallows, the other in my arms!' Cannon shots are fired and the chorus intones the *Te Deum*. After exclaiming 'Tosca, mi fai dimenticare Iddio!' – 'Tosca you make me forget God!' he joins the chorus as though awakening from a trance. With a threefold repetition of his motif (Ex. 1a) *tutta forza*, the act closes powerfully.

Act II

(Scarpia's room at the Palazzo Farnese. A table is laid for supper. A large window overlooks the courtyard of the Palazzo. Night.)

Scarpia is seated at the table, interrupting his supper from time to time to reflect on the happenings ('Reflection' motif, Ex. 1c). He frequently looks at his watch, and his whole behaviour betrays nervous tension. By now, he reckons, his agents will have arrested Angelotti and Cavaradossi, both of whom will be hanged at dawn, and Tosca will be his. The direction in which his thoughts turn is mirrored in Ex. 8 which ranges together the 'Love' theme (Ex. 4e), 'Angelotti's

Ex. 8

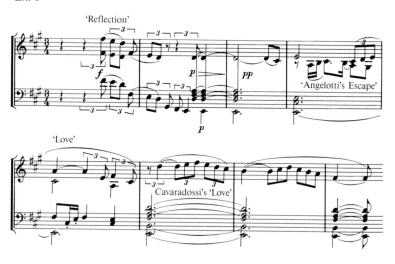

Escape' (Ex. 2c), Cavaradossi's 'Love' (4d) and the whole flanked on both sides by the 'Reflection' motif (Ex. 1c). (A similar configuration is heard a little later after Scarpia has handed a note for Tosca to Sciarrone.) Scarpia rings a bell and Sciarrone enters; Scarpia asks whether Tosca has arrived at the Palazzo to sing her cantata. At

Scarpia's order Sciarrone opens the window, and the sound of a gavotte is heard from the lower floor where a ball is taking place. Sciarrone departs with a note from Scarpia to be given to Tosca as soon as she arrives. Left alone, Scarpia launches into his erotic credo, 'Ha più forte sapore': he is not a romantic lover, he has no time for swooning sighs and sentimental serenades. A forcible conquest has for him a far keener relish than a willing surrender. He makes straight for what he desires, satiates himself and then discards his prey to turn to new conquests. God has created different beauties and different wines; he clinches his monologue with a sip of wine.

Sciarrone returns with Spoletta, who reports the outcome of his pursuit of Tosca to a little villa in the country. He has ransacked the villa from top to bottom, he says, but Angelotti could not be found. Scarpia breaks out in furious rage, threatening to send Spoletta to the gallows. Frightened, and mumbling under his breath 'God help me!', Spoletta says that Cavaradossi was at the villa after all; with every gesture and word he had expressed such mocking irony that Spoletta arrested him and brought him here. At this point the ominous 'Interrogation' march enters, here scored suggestively for two low flutes (Ex. 9a), while the sounds from Tosca's cantata float

Ex. 9a 'Interrogation' motif (march)

Ex. 9b 'Execution' motif

Ex. 10 'Pain' motif

up into the room. Scarpia orders Spoletta to bring in Cavaradossi, and the interrogation begins. The painter denies every accusation, pretending to know nothing about Angelotti, and declares it all to be the suspicion of a police spy. Annoyed and irritated by the cantata, Scarpia violently slams the window shut, so that the sound is abruptly cut off.[5] Faced with Cavaradossi's denials, Scarpia warns him that his obstinacy is not wise – 'a speedy confession will avoid much pain'; at these words the 'Pain' motif (Ex. 10) enters, *molto espressivo, lamentoso* (cellos). He asks the painter for the last time where Angelotti is to be found, at which point Tosca enters, rushes up to her lover and embraces him (Cavaradossi's 'Love', Ex. 4d). Cavaradossi manages to warn her in whisper to say nothing about what she has seen at the villa, for this would mean certain death for him. Raising his voice, Scarpia now commands Cavaradossi to be led into the torture chamber (Ex. 9a, *ff* on woodwind, horns, trumpets and first trombone) instructing the executioner Roberti to use 'first the usual form of torture. Afterwards. . . as I order.' From this point onwards the dramatic tension rises in a steady curve to the climax of Scarpia's murder.

The atmosphere for the ensuing scene (see p. 109) is set by a sombre piece in G minor as an introduction to the exchanges between Scarpia and Tosca. In order to force them to divulge Angelotti's hiding-place Scarpia plans a twofold torture for the lovers: mental for Tosca and physical for Cavaradossi. He begins his conversation with Tosca in the vein of simulated camaraderie, the music adopting the character of a smooth-flowing barcarolle in 6/8. 'Let us sit down', he says, 'and talk like good friends – no need to feel alarmed!' 'What about the fan?' 'Foolish jealousy', retorts Tosca. 'Then the Attavanti was not at the villa?' – 'Nothing escapes a jealous eye. Cavaradossi was alone', she replies. Scarpia, interrupting the conversation, calls out to Sciarrone, 'What does the *cavaliere* say?' 'Nothing', replies Sciarrone. 'Let us then continue', orders Scarpia. Tosca, as yet unaware of what is going on in the torture chamber, remarks that his interrogation of her is useless – 'must one lie in order to satisfy you?' 'No', replies Scarpia' 'but the truth could shorten a very painful hour for Cavaradossi.' (It is at these words that the 'Torture' theme (Ex. 4i) makes its first appearance.) 'A painful hour?', asks Tosca in utter surprise. It is only now that it dawns upon her that something horrible is taking place behind the closed door of the other room. In order to break her resistance, Scarpia describes how Cavaradossi, bound hand and foot, has a spiked circlet round his brow which at every further denial penetrates his flesh more deeply. Tosca, listening anxiously and hearing a prolonged moan from the closed room, is ready to speak; but first, she says, the torture must stop. On Scarpia's order the torture ceases, but Cavaradossi calls out to her to be silent – 'I scorn the pain!' This encourages her to continue denying all knowledge of Angelotti. To a new theme in D minor (*Lento grave*) in which the appoggiatura of a major ninth is the critical dissonance, Tosca, wanting to prevent Scarpia from giving the order for the resumption of the torture shouts, 'You monster, you are torturing him, killing him!' Scarpia now plays his trump card: saying with cruel irony that she has never been more tragic in the theatre, he orders the door of the torture chamber to be opened so that she may hear her lover's agonized cries of pain. Cavaradossi, however, still has the strength to shout 'I defy you!' whereupon Scarpia gives Roberti the command to intensify the torture. Tosca, seemingly at the end of her tether, breaks out into the most dramatic phrases of the opera ('Agony' motif, Ex. 11). She again implores

Ex. 11 Tosca's 'Agony' motif

Ah! più non pos-so!   Ah!___ che or-ror!   Ah!___ ces - sa-te il mar- tir!

Cavaradossi to allow her to speak, for she cannot bear it any longer; but he replies 'You silly woman! What do you know? What can you tell?' Enraged, Scarpia orders Spoletta to silence Cavaradossi. Tosca, hearing another painful cry, has reached the limit of her resistance, and betrays Angelotti's hiding-place, saying in a stifled voice, 'nel pozzo. . . nel giardino' at which the 'Well' motif (Ex. 1b) makes its reappearance. Tosca wants to see Cavaradossi, who is now brought in unconscious and covered with blood. She rushes to him, but, horrified by the sight, covers her eyes. This little scene is accompanied by an augmented version of the 'Interrogation' theme (Ex. 9a), followed by Cavaradossi's 'Love' (Ex. 4d). Coming to, he asks her if she has given away their secret – 'No, amore!' she replies. At this Scarpia calls out in a deliberately loud voice, 'In the well in the garden; go, Spoletta!', at which point the whole-tone bass of the 'Well' motif is extended a 10th from middle C down to A flat. Utterly dismayed, Cavaradossi curses Tosca. Sciarrone arrives, with hang-dog mien, announcing Napoleon's victory at the battle of Marengo. This is the

3   Act II. Maria Callas as Tosca and Tito Gobbi as Scarpia,
Covent Garden, 1964

signal for Cavaradossi to break out into a paean of liberty ('Vittoria! Vittoria!') while Tosca implores him to be silent and Scarpia breaks into a paroxysm of rage. This is set as a Trio to a rousing march-tune in B flat minor (*Allegro concitato*), which is preceded by the 'Cavaradossi' theme (Ex. 4a), here scored for trombones, while woodwind, horns and trumpets hammer out a savage rhythm, *tutta forza*. Scarpia orders Cavaradossi to be led away to be hanged.

The next scene, representing the *scène à faire* proper (see p. 110) begins with the same barcarolle-like music as Scarpia's first conversation with Tosca, but transposed to the bright key of A major which may be Puccini's way of suggesting that Scarpia feels closer to his objective. He invites Tosca to sit down at the table, offering her a glass of wine to revive her. Together, he says, they will seek a way of saving her lover's life. Tosca, looking him straight in the eye, asks after a moment's hesitation, 'Quanto? Il prezzo?' – 'How much? The price?' What kind of bargain is now revealed to her in Scarpia's monologue, 'Già. Mi dicon venal.' He does not sell himself, as he is accused, to beautiful women for money. No, if he is to betray his trust and the King of Naples he wants a different reward – Tosca herself. Her passionate embraces of Cavaradossi incited his desire for her – 'lithe as a leopard you clung to him; in that moment I swore you should be mine, mine!' (Ex. 12) (see p. 40). He advances towards her, but she takes refuge behind a settee exclaiming that she would throw herself out of the window rather than yield to him. She is suddenly struck by the idea of appealing to the Queen, but Scarpia has guessed her intention. Standing back, he calmly says: 'The Queen will pardon only a corpse!' and adding, with complacency, as Tosca fixes him with a look of utter disgust: 'How you hate me!' He again pursues her round the room, when suddenly the sound of drums is heard off-stage; it is, he explains, the sign that her lover is being led to the gallows ('Gallows' theme, Ex. 13) – he has no more than an hour to live. Leaning against the table and pouring himself a glass of wine, he coldly observes Tosca. The stage is now set for Tosca's aria, 'Vissi d'arte': her whole life has been devoted to art and love, she has never harmed a living soul, has always given secret aid to the unfortunate, offered up prayers at holy shrines and as a true believer has always laid flowers on the alter of the Madonna. 'Why has the Lord rewarded me thus?' (see p. 112).

She implores Scarpia to say a single word of mercy, her prayer being set to a theme in E flat minor marked by a dropping fifth (*come un lamento*). He seems to yield: 'Cedo. A misero prezzo tu, a me una

Ex. 12 'Lust' motif

Ex. 13 'Gallows' motif

Ex. 14 'Deception' motif

Ex. 15 'Murder' theme

vita, a te chieggo un'istante!' –'I yield. The bargain is a poor one; you ask a life of me, I, of you but a moment!', which is accompanied by the 'Lust' theme (Ex. 12). The scene is interrupted by Spoletta who brings the news that Angelotti has killed himself while they were trying to arrest him in the villa ('Angelotti' motifs, Ex. 2a and c). 'Let his corpse be hanged on the gallows.[6] And the other prisoner?' Scarpia asks. Spoletta replies that everything is made ready for the *cavaliere* Cavaradossi. 'Wait!' the Chief of Police says, and turning to Tosca softly demands 'Well?' She merely nods her consent to the infamous bargain and weeps for shame, burying her head in a cushion ('Pain' motif, Ex. 10). As Scarpia is about to give his instruction to Spoletta, Tosca interrupts him, demanding that Cavaradossi be set free on the spot. He explains that this cannot be done: a deception is necessary ('Deception' motif, Ex. 14), for everyone must believe that the *cavaliere* has been executed; in order to reassure the doubting Tosca, he gives the order to Spoletta that Cavaradossi be not hanged but shot by a firing-squad. It will be a mock-execution at 4 o'clock in the morning – 'come facemmo del conte Palmieri!' – 'as we did with Count Palmieri!' he adds meaningfully. 'Yes, as with Palmieri', repeats Spoletta, who has understood. Turning now to Tosca, Scarpia says that he has kept his side of the bargain, and he is about to embrace her when she resists – 'not yet', for she has the presence of mind to ask for a safe-conduct for herself and her lover to allow them to leave Rome unhindered. Scarpia agrees, goes to his desk and begins to write out the document. Meanwhile Tosca has approached the table in order to drink the glass of wine that Scarpia had poured out for her. In raising it to her lips her eyes fall on a knife on the table. Leaning against the table and holding behind her back the knife she has taken surreptitiously, she watches Scarpia as he finishes writing and puts his seal on the safe-conduct. All this proceeds to the melancholy theme Ex. 15 (the 'Murder') in which the sudden *f* phrase seems to indicate the moment in which her eyes fall on the knife. To his 'Lust' motif (Ex. 12), Scarpia advances on her to embrace her – 'Tosca, finalmente mia!' – but his exclamation changes into the terrible cry, 'Maledetta! Aiuto! Muoio!' – 'Curse you! Help! I am dying!': Tosca has plunged the knife into his breast. 'Questo è il bacio di Tosca!' – 'This is the kiss of Tosca!', she shouts and gloating over him, 'Are you choking in your blood? Die, you fiend, die! die!' die!' The 'Deception' motif (Ex. 14) is hammered out on woodwind and horns, as if Puccini meant to indicate that Scarpia himself has been deceived in his aim of possessing Tosca. 'He is dead! Now I forgive him!', the last sentence suggesting a psychologically unbelievably swift change of mood. Without taking her eyes off the body, she goes to the table, takes a carafe of water and dipping a table-cloth in it cleans the blood off her fingers. She suddenly remembers the safe-conduct, looks for it on the desk and cannot find it. She searches frantically elsewhere until she sees it clutched in Scarpia's hand; she takes it and hides it in her bosom. This little scene takes place to the accompaniment of theme Ex. 15. She looks again at the body and in a toneless voice (on the repeated middle C) she utters the famous phrase, 'E avanti a lui tremava tutta Roma!' She is on the point of leaving when, seized by a religious sentiment, she lights the two candles from the candelabra – the music contrasts the 'Lust' motif (Ex. 12) with Cavaradossi's 'Love' (Ex. 4d) – and places them on each side of Scarpia's head. Looking once more around the room she sees a crucifix on the wall, takes it and kneeling down before the

4 Scarpia's table

body places it on his breast. She rises and leaves, closing the door very cautiously behind her. During this stage-business the 'Scarpia' motif (Ex. 1a) concludes the Act, with its final chord in E minor. (See pp. 113–15 for discussion of this scene).

Act III

(The platform of the Castel Sant'Angelo. To the left a casemate, a table with a lamp on it, a large register, writing materials, a bench and a stool. Hung on the wall is a crucifix with a votive light in front of it. To the right, the opening of a small staircase leading up to the platform. In the background, the Vatican and St Peter's. Night. A clear sky and twinkling stars.)

By way of an *Intrada* the four horns in unison *ff* anticipate the lovers' later triumphant hymn (Ex. 4k). The curtain rises to an orchestral prelude picturing the dawn of a Roman morning (Ex. 4j) which, except for the 'Scarpia' motif stealthily flitting through it, gives no hint at all of the terrible things to come. A shepherd boy sings off-stage a sad love song ('Io de sospiri') and the bells of neighbouring churches announce the first *Ave Maria*. A gaoler enters with a lantern, lighting from it the lamp in front of the crucifix as well as that on the table. He goes back to the platform and looks down into the courtyard to see whether the escort with the prisoner has arrived. Returning to the casemate, he sits down at the table and waits, half-asleep. The following scene is accompanied by an orchestral anticipation of Cavaradossi's aria ('E lucevan le stelle'): a picket of soldiers with Cavaradossi appears on the platform, the commanding sergeant handing the gaoler a paper which the latter examines; he then opens the register and writes in it. The sergeant signs the register and departs with the picket. 'You have an hour', says the gaoler to Cavaradossi 'a priest is at your disposal'; 'No', replies Cavaradossi, but he has a last wish, this is to write a letter to 'one most dear to me', a request the gaoler grants in exchange for a ring that Cavaradossi gives him.

What passes through Cavaradossi's mind is indicated in the 'Love' theme (Ex. 4e) expressively scored for four solo cellos. (Indeed the act is full of reminiscences from the two previous acts.) He sits down to write, but is overcome by memories of Tosca and stops. Aria 'E lucevan le stelle': he recalls the hours of love which are now vanished for ever – 'Muoio disperato! E non ho amato mai tanto la vita!' – 'I die in despair! Never have I loved life so much!' (see p. 103). Tosca enters to the 'Love' theme and rushes up to him. Unable to speak for emotion she lifts his head and shows him the safe-conduct. He reads it, scarcely able to believe his eyes, saying that this must be the first mercy Scarpia has ever shown. 'And his last', adds Tosca. 'What are you saying?' interjects her surprised lover. Tosca now proceeds to tell him of Scarpia's bargain, how she prayed in vain to the Madonna and all the saints ('Tosca' theme, Ex. 4b), how she suddenly heard the ominous drums (Ex. 13), how Scarpia laughed and said to her 'You are mine!' ('Lust' motif, Ex: 12) and how she killed him (augmented version of 'Murder' theme, Ex. 15) with that knife on the table (arpeggio in the vocal part shooting up to top C). 'My hands were completely covered with blood', she adds. This is the cue for Cavaradossi's arietta 'O dolci mani mansuete e pure'. Tosca brings him back to reality, telling him that she has everything prepared for the hour of freedom – money, jewels and a carriage to take them to safety. But first, she says, he must go through the motion of a mock-execution with blank cartridges; as the firing-squad fires, he must fall down, the soldiers will retire and 'we are free'. But the thought of Cavaradossi simulating death is nagging her (Ex. 16). There follows

Ex. 16 'Instruction' motif

a love-duet, 'Amaro sol per te', in which the lovers dream of their future when 'love will be our guide on earth, our pilot on sea'. Deeply moved, they fall silent. Tosca, the more practically minded of the two, comes back to the mock-execution (Ex. 16 transposed a semitone higher). It is essential that he should fall the moment the soldiers fire, but he must be careful not to hurt himself, it is a stage trick – 'we theatrical people would know how to do it'. Cavaradossi assures her that he will fall at once and quite naturally. But he wants her to speak to him once more – 'the sound of your voice is so sweet!' For the last time they surrender to a dream of love and new hope in a triumphant hymn (Trionfal di nuova speme' Ex. 4k). As the clock stikes four, the gaoler comes to tell Cavaradossi that it is time to prepare for the execution. Tosca is inexplicably nervous. In a low voice she repeats her instruction to Cavaradossi – to fall at the first shot, to fall down properly (Ex. 16 again). 'Like Tosca in the theatre', he says to her jokingly; 'Don't joke', she admonishes him (see p. 107).

The following scene is dominated by the 'Execution' theme

(Ex. 9b) into which the 'Deception' motif (Ex. 14) is thrust at the actual firing. The firing-squad arrives, commanded by an officer who places Cavaradossi against the wall facing Tosca. The sergeant wants to blindfold him, but Cavaradossi smilingly refuses. These grim preliminaries try Tosca's patience to the utmost – 'How long this delay is! . . . I know it's only play-acting, but the suspense seems endless!' At last the soldiers load their rifles and Tosca, seeing the officer about to lower his sabre, puts her fingers into her ears so as not to hear the report. As they shoot, she gives Cavaradossi a nod to fall; he does this so naturally that it moves her to exclaim, 'What an artist!' The sergeant now inspects the body carefully and is about to give it the *coup de grâce* but is prevented by Spoletta who covers the body with a cloak. Everybody leaves except Tosca: she has been watching all these movements in fear that her lover might move or speak too soon. Finally she goes up to him to urge him to get up, but as there is no movement she touches the body and to her horror realizes that Cavaradossi is dead: Scarpia has played a fiendish trick on them both; she throws herself on his body (see p. 114–15).

From below excited shouts are heard – Scarpia's murder has been discovered. Spoletta, Sciarrone and some soldiers come up, to find Tosca prostrate over Cavaradossi's dead body. Spoletta yells that she will pay dearly for Scarpai's life; 'With my own!', she retorts. She quickly rises to her feet, pushes Spoletta so violently aside that he almost falls down the staircase, and climbs the parapet. With the words 'O Scarpia, avanti a Dio!' – 'In the presence of God, Scarpia!' she hurls herself into space; Spoletta remains rooted to the ground, horror-stricken.

The opera closes with a dramatically wholly irrelevant reminiscence of 'E lucevan le stelle', *tutta forza*, con grande slancio for nearly the whole orchestra in unison, and doubled in two octaves (see p. 115–16).

5 Play and opera: a comparison

To recast a play or a novel into an effective opera text requires a special technique. Yet, as Ernest Newman wrote some 30 years ago,[1] while there are textbooks for composers, conductors, instrumentalists and singers, there is no manual for the art of the librettist. More recently Gary Schmidgall[2] has singled out certain features in literary sources on which opera thrives, such as passionate force, lyrical expression, individuality and vigour of characters, direction of impact and simplicity. Schmidgall, however, only refers to what might be called the 'opera-genic' in literary sources – he does not touch on the *specific method* a librettist employs in translating a literary text into a viable opera text. His work appears to be entirely empirical. The good librettist is born, not made. His instinct, supported by ingenuity and technical skill, will guide him in the deployment and balancing of those features listed by Schmidgall. At the same time he must be flexible and adaptable enough to accommodate himself to the special musico-dramatic requirements of a given composer. Thus, a librettist employed by one composer will approach his task, so far as the details of his adaptation are concerned, from an angle different from that of a librettist working for another composer. Hofmannsthal could never have been the 'right' poet for Puccini, while Illica and Giacosa could never have been the right collaborators for Richard Strauss.

By common consent Illica and Giacosa were the ideal librettists for the Lucca composer and made an excellent job of the text of *Tosca*. But in the process of recasting Sardou's play they were, however, guilty of implausibilities, *faits accomplis*, insufficient motivation and omission of details that may leave the critical spectator somewhat baffled. To be sure, music has the unique power to conceal and cover up defects in the dramaturgy that would be regarded as serious, even inadmissible, in a spoken drama. It may be argued, however, that with so stageworthy and effective an opera as *Tosca* we

46

need not be as rigid and strict in our judgement of the libretto's faults as was Ernest Newman, who went so far as to declare that, dramatically, Act I of *Tosca* is an 'ill-made piece of work' that ignores motivation and explication.[3] Newman's is the extreme case of one who tends to apply the yardstick of spoken drama, in which there is time and space for detailed explanations of a character's behaviour, to opera, where by its very nature there is little time for dramaturgical niceties. Yet, given the fact that Sardou's drama is so well constructed, the concatenation of its happenings so closely forged, and the dramaturgy so beautifully crafted, it will be worthwhile to make a fairly detailed comparison between it and the libretto prepared for Puccini.

The principal tasks that faced Giacosa and Illica were reduction and, at the same time, expansion of the Sardou play: on the one hand stripping it down to its dramatic essentials and, on the other, stretching it in order to make room for lyrical episodes of which there were none in Sardou but which were a *conditio sine qua non* for Puccini's operatic dialectics (see p. 91). Let us deal first with the reductions.

La Tosca is in five acts and has 23 speaking roles – *Tosca* has three acts and nine singing characters. The play's historico-political background is impressively sketched in Act II in which Sardou introduces such personalities as Queen Maria Luisa of Naples (a sister of Marie Antoinette), the Austrian General Fröhlich and the composer Paisiello. Moreover, the drama unfolds in such historical and still extant localities as the Church of Sant'Andrea della Valle (actually Sant'Andrea al Quirinale), the Palazzo Farnese and the Castel Sant'Angelo, which was once a papal fortress. Sardou also fixes the exact date on which the action takes place – 'Rome, 17 June 1800' (Puccini has simply 'June 1800').[4] This mixture of historical data by which the French playwright lent his drama a veneer of authenticity, with a fictitious plot and characters, was a characteristic feature of his dramatic style. Now, a fair amount of this background, considered by Puccini as superfluous trappings anyhow, could be disposed of, without detriment to the drama between Scarpia, Tosca and Cavaradossi. Hence Sardou's Act II, which in the main was a grand scenic spectacle, was all but completely excised. What was retained from it was the festive cantata in celebration of General Melas's supposed victory over the French, which is never performed in the play, however, since the news brought to the Queen of the Austrians' defeat by Napoleon throws the august assembly into disarray and all the guests leave the Palazzo in utter confusion. In

Puccini's Act II the cantata *is* performed and provides the musical background for Cavaradossi's interrogation. This was a master-stroke on the part of Puccini's librettists as, apart from the strong musical contrast it creates, it serves to illuminate simultaneously the two extremes of the royalist regime: on the one hand its pomp and circumstance (the cantata), on the other the persecution of its political enemies (the interrogation of Cavaradossi). The other element retained from Sardou's Act II was Scarpia's idea of using the fan in order to a rouse Tosca's jealousy, so making her the decoy who will lead his agents to Angelotti's hide-out. This was transferred to Act I of the opera. In addition, events that Sardou distributed over his Act III (Cavaradossi's villa) and Act IV (Scarpia's room in the Castel Sant'Angelo) in order to achieve a *gradual* mounting of the tension were telescoped into Puccini's Act II, set in the Palazzo Farnese, with the result that the accumulation of such 'strong' situations as Cavaradossi's torture, Scarpia's attempted rape of Tosca, his bargain with her, and finally his murder, makes that act at once the most spine-chilling and most powerful of the three acts. This *Ballung*, or accumulation, conformed wholly to the dramaturgy of verismo. Lastly, Sardou's Act V consists of two scenes, the first laid in the prisoner's cell, and the second on the platform of the Castel Sant'Angelo. The reason for what may at first seem an unnecessary delay was evidently twofold. First, it shows Cavaradossi's anti-clericalism, for he refuses the offer of all religious rites before his execution – 'Je vous en prie, capitaine, épargnez-moi leurs instances inutiles et leurs chants lugubres' – 'I beg you, captain, spare me their [the white monks] useless prayers and mournful chanting', whereas in the opera Cavaradossi simply says 'No'. Second, it gives Tosca (as played by Sarah Bernhardt) a solo scene in which to display, after her lover has been led off to the platform, her extreme agitation while awaiting the sound of the simulated execution – 'C'est odieuse cette attente! . . . cela serre le coeur . . . j'ai beau savoir que ce n'est qu'un jeu . . . la pensée qu'on va tirer sur lui! Ah, mon Dieu!' – 'This waiting is terrible! . . . It's heart-rending . . . It's no use that I know it is only play-acting . . . The thought that they will fire on him! O, my God!'

These two scenes were fused into one as Act III of the opera which, apart from shortening the text, has this advantage: the spectator witnesses Tosca *seeing* the preparation for and the execution itself, while in Sardou she only *hears* it in the distance. The gain of this compression is that the spectator experiences one of the few moments in the opera in which he feels true compassion for the heroine, for he knows that it will be a real execution whereas she still thinks that it will be simulated. It is the knowledge of this deception that touches our hearts.

There are two further important alterations in Puccini, both occurring in Act I and both resulting in a considerable tightening-up of Sardou's text. The play opens with a long conversation between Eusèbe the Sacristan and Cavaradossi's young valet, Gennarino, in which we learn about the painter's family background as well as about the Sacristan's religious bigotry and his strong royalist leanings. All this is overheard by Angelotti who has been hiding in the Angelotti Chapel (in Puccini it is the Attavanti Chapel) since the evening before the action starts. In the opera, on the other hand, we are catapulted *in medias res* when we see Angelotti arriving at the church in a state of utter fear and nervous agitation, which at one stroke does away with Sardou's lengthy conversation between Eusèbe and Gennarino. Puccini's second alteration concerns the relationship between Angelotti and Cavaradossi. In the play Angelotti has never met Cavaradossi before, but from the Sacristan's conversation one gathers that Cavaradossi is, like Angelotti, an anti-royalist with strong republican sympathies. Yet, as the two men are complete strangers to each other, when they meet they have to introduce themselves and so a long dialogue develops, in the course of which we learn Angelotti's turbulent life story. But what is possible in a play is not possible in an opera. Puccini's librettists eliminated this dialogue by the simple expedient of having Cavaradossi know Angelotti from his past, so that a mutual introduction is no longer necessary. All that Angelotti tells the painter is the reason for his hiding in the Attavanti Chapel. Is it therefore acceptable to speak of Act I of *Tosca* as an 'ill-made piece of work' as Newman did? There is little doubt that the majority of these dramaturgical improvements in the libretto were made with Sardou's consent – some may even have been suggested by the playwright himself. There is a grain of truth in Sardou's later declaration that from a purely dramatic point of view the libretto was superior to his play.

What both play and opera share in common are the classical unities of time, place and action, which in Puccini are even more strictly observed through the elimination of Sardou's spectacular Act II. The action takes place in Rome within the space of twelve hours, and the plot unfolds in a straight line to the very end. This serves to heighten, albeit subliminally, the spectator's impression of utmost concentration in the opera's dramaturgy. And this is to say nothing of the oppressive sense of claustrophobia which emanates from the opera, each act playing in an enclosed space.

I now come to the expansion of the Sardou text necessitated by the need for lyrical episodes which, as I remarked, are completely missing in the play and for which an entirely fresh text had to be written. These lyrical enclaves are almost invariably in rhymed verse in irregular metre. Two such enclaves are to be found in Act I – Cavaradossi's aria 'Recondita armonia' and the great love scene. What is also new is Scarpia's monologue in the finale of the act, which is quite different from what he says in the play. Act II has three lyrical insertions – Scarpia's erotic credo 'Ha più forte sapore' and his 'Già. Mi dicon venal', though it is perhaps hardly appropriate to call this second piece lyrical when the character sings himself into a frenzy of lust and is about to do violence to the heroine. There follows Tosca's famous aria 'Vissi d'arte' which Puccini later thought dramatically superfluous since, he argued, it held up the action, and which he wanted to abolish altogether. If we disregard the Shepherd Boy's little love-song in the Prelude, Act III contains two lyrical pieces, Cavaradossi's lament 'E lucevan le stelle' and the love scene, opening with 'O dolci mani'. Most of these insertions will be discussed in detail in the analytical section of the book.

If Puccini's compression of Sardou's play considerably concentrated the action, these improvements were bought at a price. In his concern for the condensation of the French original to its dramatic essentials the composer overshot his mark, and eliminated dramaturgical and psychological elements needed to make certain points in the action comprehensible, and for presenting the characters more in the round. In this Puccini was not alone. Over-compression was also the weakness of Verdi's dramaturgy and, indeed, of every opera composer dealing with a subject drawn from a spoken drama. Not that the spectator needs much detailed explanation, which is impossible in opera, where in addition to the generally retarding effect of music, there is a limit to what the audience is able to understand of the sung words. But Puccini's librettists might have retained more of Sardou's careful sketching of the historical background and of details about the characters. What for instance is the critical spectator to make of Cavaradossi's exclamation 'The Consul of the ill-fated Roman Republic!' when he first sees Angelotti, and of his 'You can count on me!' after Angelotti has told him that he has just escaped from the Castel Sant'Angelo? Or, how does it come about that Scarpia, in his pursuit of Angelotti, comes straight from the papal fortress to the church of Sant'Andrea della Valle? Do we have to credit the Roman

Chief of Police with an acumen that would do honour to Sherlock Holmes? Finally, how do we square Cavaradossi's sudden outburst of revolutionary fervour in Act II with the fact that up to then Puccini has not given us the slightest hint that Tosca's lover is a political animal? For a full appreciation of *Tosca* it is desirable that the spectator should know more about the protagonists than the composer has vouchsafed him and that he should have Sardou's play at the back of his mind - as Puccini did. It is only then that implausible and unexplained aspects of the opera fall into place and make sense. The filling of these gaps will, it is hoped, also be of use to the producer, conductor and singers in the interpretation of the opera.

The character who first claims our attention is Scarpia - psychologically the most fascinating of the three protagonists. In Sardou he has the cognomen 'Vitellio', dropped by Puccini's librettists for the evident reason that there is at once more force and a more sinister ring in the single name 'Scarpia'. (The Italian *scarificare* - to scarify - comes to mind.) Scarpia comes from Sicily, the traditional land of the Mafia[5] and it is significant that when in the play Angelotti mentions his name he refers in the same breath to the Neapolitan brigands Fra Diavolo and Mammone 'who cut the throats of their prisoners'. At the time of the action Scarpia has been in Rome not more than a week, having been sent by the King of Naples to keep an iron grip on the republicans. In Sardou he is portrayed as though he had stepped out of the Spanish Inquisition - a fanatic and an utterly ruthless and brutal zealot who hides his true nature - sadistic lechery - behind a mask of sanctimoniousness and religious piety. In Puccini he is the more traditional stage villain, but his brutality is toned down, and when expedient he can appear smooth, suave and mellifluous - in short as an *homme du monde*. After all, he is Baron Scarpia - an aristocrat (often overlooked in the interpretation of this role). It is noteworthy that in the play the motive that drives Scarpia to pursue Angelotti relentlessly is a very personal one. As the Queen warns him, a week has gone by since his arrival in Rome and already Angelotti, a political prisoner at the Castel Sant'Angelo, has made his successful escape. Rumours, the Queen says, are making the rounds in the city that this escape might not be unconnected with the fact that Angelotti's sister happens to be the Marchesa Attavanti - 'a wealthy and beautiful woman', she adds meaningfully. If Scarpia cannot hunt down Angelotti soon, his own head, she gives him to understand, may be at stake. There is no hint of this in Puccini.

Moreover, it is not until Act IV of the play that Scarpia reveals himself as the satyr he is; up to then he has conducted himself *vis à vis* Tosca with the cold, formal and detached air of a high police official who, in suppressing dangerous subversive elements, is only doing his duty by the king. Indeed, at the end of Act III he gives the order that Cavaradossi *as well as* Tosca is to be hanged. (When Scarpia commands Sciarrone to take the painter to the gallows, the latter asks, 'Et la femme?'; Scarpia replies, 'La femme aussi!' Curtain. But in Act IV he changes his mind saying to Tosca that it would not please God to deprive the Romans of their idol, who is also his idol. He will let her go free). Puccini, forced as he was to compress the play, had inevitably to forgo a finely shaded portrayal and introduces Scarpia already in Act I as a compound of religious bigot, lecher and high state official. It is interesting to compare how Cavaradossi describes him in the play and in the opera:

Sardou	Puccini
Ah, wretch! Under the mask of perfect politeness and fervent religious devotion, with his smiles and signs of the cross, that vile scoundrel, hypocritical and corrupt, an artist in wickedness in his villainy, bloody even in his orgies! What woman – daughter or sister – has not paid with her virtue when she intervened with this abominable satyr?	Scarpia? A bigoted satyr who under the cover of devout practice indulges his lecherous desires, and to serve his voracious appetite acts as both confessor and executioner!

Sardou's description is plainly too elaborate to be used in its entirety in the libretto, but the sentence, 'What woman – daughter or sister – has not paid . . .' might have been easily added to Puccini's text to lend it a sharper edge.

In his *scène à faire* (Act IV), Sardou pulls out all the stops to show Scarpia in his frenzied lust and sexual sadism in which, as the Sardou excerpt quoted on p. 53 makes clear, there is also a large measure of sexual envy and jealousy of Tosca's lover. (There is only a slight hint of this in the opera.) Given Puccini's psychological make-up, it might be assumed that this scene struck a deep chord in his unconscious fantasies. Yet he held back (as he did in the case of the abortive libretto drawn from Pierre Louÿs's sex novel, *La femme et le pantin*) and did not give Scarpia the same degree of violence and frenzy as in the original. Apart from considerably shortening Sardou's text, he toned down its ferocious language and introduced a further emollient in Scarpia's quasi-lyrical monologue. To illustrate the difference as well as the skill of Puccini's librettists in condensing and lyricizing the original, I print the two texts side by side:

Sardou	Puccini
Scarpia: Now then! Pray be seated! A glass of Spanish wine! (*He pours it out.*) In this way we shall feel more at ease as we talk about the Chevalier and find a means to extricate him from this bad business.	Scarpia (*calm and smiling*): My poor supper was interrupted. Why so alarmed? Come, lovely lady, sit down here. Shall we together find some way of saving him? Be seated and we'll talk it over. Meanwhile a glass of Spanish wine. A sip will raise your spirits.
Tosca: I'm not thirsty nor hungry – except for his freedom! . . . Well now, to the point! (*She resolutely takes a seat at Scarpia's table and pushes the glass away.*) How much?	Tosca (*contemptuously*): How much?
S. (*pouring out*): How much? T.: It's a question of money, isn't it? S.: Shame on you, Tosca! You don't know me at all . . . Yes, you have seen me fierce and implacable when I discharged my duty; that was because my honour and life are at stake: Angelotti's escape has brought disgrace on me – inevitably. But once my duty is done I'm like a soldier who is no longer an enemy when he discards his weapon. Before you stands Baron Scarpia who has always applauded you and admired you to the point of fanaticism. But tonight my admiration has taken on a new character. Yes, up to now, I saw in you only the great interpreter of Cimarosa and Paisiello. But our contretemps has revealed the woman in you, a woman more tragic, more pas-	S.: How much? T.: What's your price? S. (*monologue*): Yes, they say I'm venal, but I don't sell myself for money to lovely women. If I

sionate than the artist ever led me to believe, and a hundred times more admirable in the love and pains of real life than you are on the stage! Ah, Tosca, you found such accents, cries, gestures, attitudes! . . . No, it was prodigious. I was impressed to the point of forgetting my proper role in this tragedy. I would have applauded you simply as a spectator and declared myself conquered by you!

T. (*still ill at ease, under her breath*): Would to God it were so!
S.: But do you known what held me back? In all my enthusiasm for you who fascinate and intoxicate me, who are so different from all those women who have been mine, there is jealousy, a sudden jealousy. It bites into my heart. Fancy, all those rages and tears for that Chevalier who, between ourselves, is not worth so much passion! Ah! The more you plead for him, the more you strengthen in me an obstinate urge to keep him in my power and make him expiate so much love. Yes, upon my word, I want to punish him for it! I hate him because his luck is undeserved. I envy him the possession of a woman like you to such an extent that I shall not let him free, except on one condition – to get my share!
T. (*leaping from her seat*): You!
S. (*still seated, holds her back by the arm*): And I shall get it!
T. (*bursting out into laughter, while she violently tries to free herself*): You imbecile! I would rather throw myself out of the window!

have to betray my sworn duty I choose a different payment. I have been waiting for this hour. Love of the diva has long consumed me! But a little while ago I saw you as I have never seen you before! Your tears flowed like lava on my senses, and your eyes, which are arrows of hate, made my desire all the fiercer. When, agile as a leopard, you embraced your lover, ah, in that moment I swore you will be mine!

T. (*horrified*): Ah! Ah!
S.: Wholly mine! Wholly mine!

T.: No! I would rather throw myself out of the window!

S. (*without stirring, coldly*): All right! Your lover will follow you! Say 'yes' and I'll save him – 'no' and I'll kill him.

T. (*looking at him, horrified*): You abominable scoundrel! What a horrible bargain by means of brute force and terror!

S.: *Bon, ma chère*, but why this violent language? If the bargain doesn't suit you, well, go then! – you will scream, insult me, invoke the Holy Virgin and all the saints! Waste time with useless words! After that you will say 'yes'!

T.: Never! I shall wake the whole town and shout out your infamy.

S. (*sipping his wine, coldly*): That won't wake the dead! (*Tosca stops short with a gesture of despair.*) You hate me very much, don't you?

T.: O God!

S. (*as before*): Well and good! I'll tell you how I love you. (*He puts the wine-glass down on the table.*) A woman who gives herself willingly is not worth speaking of. I have had my fill of those! (*He advances towards Tosca.*) But to humiliate you, for all your scorn and rage, to break your resistance and twist you in my arms – by God, that's where the savour of it lies. It would only spoil the feast for me if you submitted!

T. (*leaning with her back against Scarpia's writing-desk*): You demon!

S. (*with one knee on the settee*): Demon? Be it so! What fascinates me, you haughty creature, is that you should be mine in all your rage and pain –

S.: Your Mario remains my hostage.

T.: Ah, you fiend! What a horrible bargain!

(*The idea of appealing to the Queen strikes her and she runs towards the door.*)

S. (*divining her thoughts*): I will not force you to stay. You are free to go. But your hope is an illusion. The Queen would pardon a corpse. How you hate me!

T.: O God!

T.: Don't touch me, you demon! I hate and detest you, you vile, despicable creature!

S.: What matter! Hatred and love are kindred passions!

that I should feel the struggle and shock in your soul – feel how your unwilling body shudders at the caresses forced on it – how your flesh is the slave of my flesh! What a revenge for your insults and what a refinement of voluptuousness that my pleasure should be your punishment. Ah, you hate me! But I, I want you. I promise myself a diabolic enjoyment from the union of my lust and your hatred!

T. (*goes to the table*): Of what union were you born, you savage beast! It couldn't have been the breast of a woman who suckled you!

T.: You beast!

S. (*advancing towards her*): Go on! Continue! Insult me! Spit your contempt into my face, bite and tear me! All this only whips up my desire and makes me covet you still more!

S. (*trying to seize her*): Mine!

T. (*trying to escape, terrified*): Help, help!

S.: No one will come! You only waste your time with useless shrieks. Look, it's getting brighter and your Mario has not more than a quarter of an hour to live!

(*Tosca shrieks for help. Distant drums are heard.*)
S.: Do you hear? It's the drums accompanying the escort of the condemned on their last journey. (*Pointing to the window.*) There they are raising the gallows. It is your will then that your Mario shall die in a mere hour?
Tosca's aria 'Vissi d'arte'

T.: Oh Almighty! God the Saviour! That such a man should live and that You should allow him to do these things! Do You not see him! Do You not hear him?

S. (*jeeringly*): Ha! If you count on Him! . . . Angelotti hangs already on the gibbet (*Tosca draws back in horror*). It's now the turn of the other! (*calling*) Spoletta!

T. (*rushing to the window*): No, no! Save him!

S. (*takes her by the hand and is about to embrace her*): Do you consent?

T. (*slips out of his arms and throws herself at his feet*): Pity! Mercy! Oh God! You've had your revenge! I've been punished and humiliated enough. I lie at your feet. I beseech you. I implore you to forgive me for all I said. I am humble now. Have pity on me! Pity!

T.: Must I kneel and beg for pity? Look, I beseech you with folded hands. See, here I am, humbled, pleading for one word of pity.

S.: Well then! We're agreed, aren't we? (*He lifts her up and tries again to embrace her.*)

S.: Tosca, you are too lovely, and too enchanting, I yield. It's a poor bargain: you ask of me a life, I ask of you but a moment!

T. (*frees herself with a cry of disgust*): No, no! I don't want to! I couldn't! I don't want to!

T. (*scornfully*): Go, go! You make me shudder! (*There is a knock at the door.*)

S.: Who is there?

Enter Spoletta

The distant drum rolls in Puccini's dialogue (p. 56) merit a brief comment. They are not in Sardou. Puccini, by introducing the ominous sound in reply, as it were, to Tosca's futile shrieks for help, together with Scarpia's explanatory words, not only heightens the emotional tension at a crucial psychological moment, but also provides a highly dramatic motivation for Tosca's subsequent 'Vissi d'arte', the lyrical high-point of the act. It is in such details that Puccini's dramatic instinct manifests itself to admirable effect.

The Tosca of the play appears as a somewhat grander, more imperious figure than her operatic counterpart. She is there a real *prima donna assoluta* throwing tantrums at the slightest provocation and no respecter of persons, not even of the Queen of Naples. When in Sardou's Act II her jealousy has been roused by Scarpia's insinuation about her lover, she is prepared to let the cantata go to perdition, Queen or no Queen, and rush off to Cavaradossi's villa and surprise him with the Marchesa Attavanti. To show her as a spoiled diva, Sardou introduces in that act a little scene between her and Paisiello. They are about to begin the cantata when this dialogue ensues:

Paisiello: Are you ready, diva?
Tosca: Yes, yes, I am ready. Let's get on quickly!
P.: B natural, isn't it?
T.: No, B flat!
P.: Oh!
T. (*violently*): B flat!

P. (*turning to the orchestra*): B flat! B flat! Gentlemen! (*At that moment the Queen arrives, taking her time to get to her seat*)
T. (*sotto voce*): Good God! When is she going to sit down, that Queen? (*The Queen takes her seat*) At last!
P. (*to Tosca*): Maestoso?
T.: Yes!
P.: Largo . . . Largo.
T.: You bore me.
P.: Yes, charming lady! (*To Scarpia*) She has her nerves, you know!
S.: Yes, a little.
P.: Let us begin, gentlemen!

Sardou has given us all the details of Tosca's rise to fame. Born in the Roman Campagna, she began her life as a wild, untamed creature tending the goats in the fields until the Benedictine nuns of Verona took pity on her and brought her up in their convent. Hence Tosca's devout piety, which stands in such strong contrast to Cavaradossi's free-thinking attitude. In the convent she began to take singing lessons from the organist, displaying so unusual a gift that at the age of sixteen she was already a youthful celebrity. It was then that the great Cimarosa heard her and tried to remove her from the convent in order to make an opera singer of her. A fierce tug-of-war for Tosca's soul ensued between the nuns and the composer, and the Pope himself was appealed to as a final arbiter. At an 'audition' at the Vatican the Pope was so moved by her singing that he declared her free to devote herself to an artistic career – 'You will soften all hearts as you have softened mine. You will make people shed gentle tears, and that is also a way of praying to God.' Tosca's operatic début was in Paisiello's *Nina* at La Scala, then came the San Carlo in Naples and La Fenice in Venice. At the time of the action she is thrilling her audiences at the Argentina in Rome, where Cavaradossi has met her and fallen in love with her at first sight.

In the opening act of both play and opera Tosca's mood changes like a weathercock, being in turn quick-tempered, suspicious, amorous, coquettish and above all insanely jealous and devoutly religious. 'These are her two great faults' says Cavaradossi to Angelotti, although her piety has not prevented her from 'living in sin' (to use a now obsolescent phrase) with her lover. (This is a nice paradox by which Sardou takes account of the susceptibilities both of the Catholic and of the liberal, more free-thinking, sections of the French people.) Tosca, we learn, hides nothing from her father confessor, who has denounced her love for Cavaradossi as abominable and adjures her to convert him to a religious life, for then God will pardon her sin. As a first sign of this conversion, the good father says, she ought to persuade Cavaradossi to get rid of his – imperial: it is the emblem of a godless revolutionary. Cavaradossi informs Angelotti that, being an ardent royalist, she might betray the fugitive to the authorities since she regards him as an 'enemy of God, the King and the Pope'. It is wiser, the painter argues, not to let her into the secret of Angelotti's escape – 'the only discreet woman is the one who knows nothing'. As for Tosca's strong religious feeling, this is stressed in both play and opera, notably in the ceremony she performs after killing Scarpia, but it is underlined in Puccini still more by Tosca's second-act aria 'Vissi d'arte' and by the last words she utters before hurling herself from the parapet of Sant'Angelo at the end of Act III – 'O Scarpia avanti a Dio!' – 'Scarpia, God will be our judge!', which is a far cry from Tosca's parting-shot in Sardou – 'J'y vais, canailles!'

In the course of the action, of both play and opera, Tosca shows a measure of psychological development, in that she grows from the featherhead of the opening to the later heroine – prepared to sacrifice her honour for her lover's liberty, possessing the presence of mind to ask Scarpia for the safe-conduct and not hesitating to kill him when she perceives the knife on the table. As Cavaradossi exclaims after she has told him (Act V of the play) of the murder of Scarpia, 'Ah, vaillante femme! Tu es bien une Romaine, une vraie Romaine d'autrefois!' – 'Courageous woman! You are a true Roman, a Roman of ancient times!' Sardou's allusion to the old Romans is intended to emphasize her heroic deed; it was replaced in Puccini by Cavaradossi's more personal line, 'Tu? di tua mano l'uccidesti! – tu pia, tu benigna, e per me!' – 'You? With your own hands you killed him! You, so pious and kind, and for me!' To this the librettists make Tosca reply, 'N'ebbi le mani tutte lorde di sangue!' – 'My hands were covered with blood' – which, quite naturally, leads to the duet 'O dolci mani' – 'O sweet hands'. This unforced transition to the love duet shows the skill of Puccini's librettists when they were dealing with situations of their own invention. (There is no corresponding love scene in Sardou.) But I feel that in the finale of the opera they let Puccini down in one important instance. Admittedly, Sardou's last scene could not have been taken over as it stood; for one thing, it was too long for Puccini's purpose, and for another there was his concern over the language that Sardou puts at that moment into Tosca's mouth – language that shows her gloating, almost sadistically, over the manner in which she killed Scarpia (which may have alienated the audience's sympathy for the heroine) and that was too realistic into the bargain. When in the play Tosca realizes the horrible deception Scarpia has played on her, she is seized by a murderous fury and, shouting to Spoletta and the others, says that it was she who killed Scarpia:

Oui, j'ai tué votre Scarpia! Tué, tué, entendez-vous? D'un coup de couteau dans le coeur, et je voudrais encore l'y plonger et l'y tordre! Ah! vous fusillez . . . moi, j'égorge! . . . Oui, allez . . . allez voir *ce que j'ai fait de ce monstre dont le cadavre assassine encore* . . . J'y vais, canailles!

(Yes, I've killed your Scarpia! Killed him, killed him, do you hear? With a knife in his heart, and I would plunge it in again and twist it there! . . . Oh, you kill with the gun! I kill with the knife! . . . Yes, go and see *what I have done to that monster whose corpse can still commit murder* . . . You shall not have me, you scum!)

Sardou's penultimate line (which I print in italics) is important because it implies that Scarpia's powers are so great that they extend beyond his death. This line was omitted by the librettists, and I shall show in the analytical section that, had it been included in Puccini's text, it might have induced him to find a different and dramatically more relevant ending to the opera than we have now.

As for the Cavaradossi of the play, he is at once a more mature and more articulate character than the impulsive and reckless painter of the opera. To this extent Giacosa's contemptuous dismissal of the operatic hero as simply *il signor tenore* seems justified. Owing to the compression of the French text, Puccini's librettists were compelled to leave out all detail about Cavaradossi's background, especially his strong sympathies for the republican cause. There is only a vague hint at this in what Scarpia says when the Sacristan mentions Cavaradossi's name, 'Lui! L'amante di Tosca! Un uom sospetto! Un volterrian!' – 'He! The lover of Tosca! A man under suspicion! A Voltairean!' This can scarcely be accepted as a sufficient retroactive explanation for Cavaradossi's earlier exclamation, 'Il Consul della spenta repubblica romana!' and 'Disponete di me!' when he recognizes Angelotti (Act I). To understand this and other unexplained things we have to turn to Sardou's play.

There we learn that Cavaradossi is the scion of an ancient family of Roman patricians who inherited his great wealth as well as his republican outlook from his father. The latter lived in Paris where he frequented the circle of the *philosophes* (the *encyclopédistes* Diderot and D'Alembert) and was also a friend of Voltaire, the arch-enemy of the Catholic Church. Cavaradossi's mother was French and the great-niece of the philosopher Helvétius. He was brought up in Paris during the time of the French Revolution and worked in the studio of the great Ferdinand David. Family affairs have brought him to Rome where the chief reason for his prolonged stay is Tosca, whom he first met a year before the action of the play starts. Cavaradossi is an intellectual (of which nothing appears in Puccini's opera) who tries to educate the untutored, unsophisticated Tosca. For example, he had given her Rousseau's *La Nouvelle Héloïse* to read; and when her father confessor heard of this, he offered her the choice either of burning it or being burnt herself in hell. Her own disapproval of the novel is not due to religious scruple but to the fact that the characters bore her – they talk much about love but practise it too little. Soon Cavaradossi and Tosca will be leaving, for her to fulfil a season's engagement at La Fenice in Venice; they will have turned their back on Rome for ever. Rome is not a safe place for him because, though he has not actually engaged in subversive activity, he is in bad odour with the Roman authorities for his known republican sympathies. Moreover, he dresses in the French style and wears an imperial which, as Sardou's Eusèbe remarks, is the sure sign of an – atheist. In Sardou's Act V there is a little scene between Spoletta and Cavaradossi in which the latter cynically refuses all religious comfort before his execution. In the libretto this scene is reduced to the painter's declining the offer with a simple 'No'. This was done in order not to offend against the religious susceptibilities of the Italian public, though Cavaradossi's atheism was largely shared by Puccini himself. But, given this attitude, how does it come about that Cavaradossi is painting a picture of Mary Magdalene in the church? Sardou gives us the answer. As the painter explains to Angelotti, this is simply a ruse: he has offered the Jesuit Order his services (in the play it is the Church of the Jesuits built by Bernini) in order to mislead the authorities as to his true political convictions. In the opera we are scarcely made aware of these convictions. For this reason, his sudden outburst of revolutionary enthusiasm when the news of Napoleon's victory at Marengo is brought to Scarpia (Act II) comes as a complete surprise. Moreover, sticklers for psychological credibility are bound to balk at the fact that Cavaradossi, who had a moment or two previously been carried from the torture chamber into Scarpia's room in a state of utter physical and mental exhaustion, should suddenly find the strength to break out, *con grande entusiasmo*, into a paean about freedom and in the course of it to deliver himself of a top B flat and several high A flats. This is, however, about the only place in the opera where operatic conventions get the better of Puccini the dramatist.

In conclusion one point must be mentioned which has escaped all commentators including myself, and to which I was alerted by Tito Gobbi's article (p. 87). In Sardou there is no hint that Cavaradossi might suspect that he will never escape from Scarpia's clutches or that his execution will be real not sham. Puccini here (Act III) introduces a scarcely perceptible subtlety by suggesting that Cavaradossi considers himself doomed. For when Tosca admonishes him to fall the moment the soldiers shoot, his reply is, 'Non temere che cadrò sul momento e al naturale' – 'Have no fear! I shall fall at once and quite naturally'. Over this phrase the composer wrote in brackets '*triste*'; whereas if Cavaradossi really thinks the execution is simulated he would be full of elation. What follows confirms his premonition. For why should he ask Tosca to speak to him once more as she has just spoken – 'the sound of your voice is so sweet' – if in a few moments he will be free and united with Tosca for ever? His last words, 'tua voce', are set to a dropping fifth (F sharp–B), this interval in Puccini being almost invariably associated with the idea of despair and death.

We come finally to Angelotti. In the drama he is no more than an episodic figure, but he is its *raison d'être*. His escape brings Scarpia on the scene, and thus sets the essential action in motion. All the information that Puccini's librettists vouchsafe us about Angelotti is that at one time he had been the Consul of the defunct Roman Republic, that he was arrested by the royalists and thrown into the Castel Saint'Angelo as a political prisoner, and, thanks to his sister's help, has made his escape to the church of Sant'Andrea della Valle. In order to fill out this vague portrait of Angelotti we again turn to Sardou. In the opening act of the play we learn that he is the descendant of an ancient family of Roman nobles, a member of which was the founder of the Church of the Jesuits (Sant'Andrea della Valle in the opera) where the family has its own chapel – the Angelotti Chapel. Like Cavaradossi, Angelotti is a republican, but unlike Cavaradossi he has openly engaged in political activities in the so-called Parthenopean Republic of Naples, one of the several republics Napoleon established in Italy in 1798–9. Driven out of Naples by the Bourbon king Ferdinand IV, he fled to Rome where he had been made Consul of the Roman Republic. But with the establishment of the Kingdom of the Two Sicilies and with the assistance of the British fleet under Admiral Nelson the Republic was suppressed and Angelotti's name put on the proscribed list. He was subsequently caught and incarcerated in the papal fortress of Sant'Angelo but could not be formally charged, since Pope Pius VI was himself a prisoner in France; thanks to his sister's influence Angelotti became a 'forgotten' prisoner who, it was hoped, would receive an amnesty on the installation of a new Pope, Pius VII. The court of Naples, however, has recently despatched the fearsome Baron Scarpia to Rome, a notorious *courreur des femmes* reputed to have been the lover of the Queen of Naples and who has had his eye also on the Marchesa Attavanti. Scarpia has instituted a reign of terror in Rome, and, fearing a move by the Attavanti to set her brother free, has decided to send Angelotti back to Naples for swift execution.[6] The Attavanti, however, has forestalled Scarpia by bribing her brother's gaoler, one Trebelli, to assist Angelotti's escape from his cell to the church in disguise. She has given the gaoler the only key to the Angelotti Chapel where during repeated visits she has managed to hide women's clothing, a fan and other articles, to enable her brother to flee from the church dressed as a woman and to join her at Frascati. Discovering that Angelotti's cell at Sant' Angelo was empty, Scarpia arrested the gaoler who under torture had disclosed Angelotti's escape plan. This explains why Scarpia has been able to make straight from the papal fortress to the church of Sant'Andrea della Valle, which in the opera remains a complete puzzle. Another implausibility in Puccini, namely the fact that Angelotti arrives at the church in *prisoner's garb* (expressly indicated in the stage direction) and, presumably, in full daylight when he must run the risk of being immediately recognized as an escaped prisoner, is better managed in Sardou: Angelotti had already changed into ordinary clothes in his cell at Sant'Angelo. It seems probable that Sardou modelled this character after an historical figure, the famed Roman surgeon, Liborio Angelucci.[7]

Nor is the Sacristan, a wholly negligible figure, merely introduced to provide comic relief. Apart from his remarks about Cavaradossi, from which we gather something about the painter's atheism, his greed for food (Cavaradossi's food basket!) leads Scarpia to suspect that Angelotti had been in the church and that Tosca's lover is his accomplice.

6   First production and critical history

With the action of the opera set in Rome, Ricordi's choice (first suggested by Illica) of the Italian capital for the first production was as appropriate as it was diplomatic, since it was calculated to flatter the Roman public's *amour propre* as well as its local patriotism. But evidently the publisher had not reckoned with two things. The first was the implied anti-clericalism of the opera manifest not only in Cavaradossi but also in the fact that its villain was himself portrayed as a devout believer; this threw an odd light on the Catholic Church and would probably go against the grain of many spectators, to say nothing of the Vatican. The second thing likely to have an adverse influence on the opera's reception was the traditional antagonism that existed (and seems still to exist) between Rome and the cities of northern Italy. But what Ricordi could not foresee was that the disturbed political atmosphere of the time would greatly contribute to the nervous tension that reigned at the Teatro Costanzi on the evening of the first night – 14 January 1900. There was, incidentally, a notable coincidence: ten years earlier Mascagni had launched at the same theatre his *Cavalleria rusticana*, which marked the birth of verismo.

   The three principal roles were taken by Hariclée Darclée (Tosca), Emilio De Marchi (Cavaradossi) and Eugenio Giraldoni (Scarpia). Darclée seems to have been chosen for the part less for her vocal accomplishments than for her striking beauty and her talent as an actress. She and her two partners belonged to the rising school of actor–singers which was beginning to emerge in response to the histrionic demands made on the performers of realist operas. Instead of the rather stiff and static acting cultivated by the older generation of singers, the cast of *Tosca* favoured a more lively, more flexible and altogether more dynamic style of acting. Incidentally, the costume in which the heroine appears in Act I has much changed since those early days. Darclée and subsequent interpreters of the part continued

64

5 Signed photograph of the first Tosca, Hariclée Darclée

to wear the style of dress that Sarah Bernhardt introduced in 1887 and that Sardou's stage direction demanded: a rustling silk dress, a large plumed hat, a long cane and a bouquet of flowers. Modern productions, however, in conformity with present taste, aim at greater simplicity, and dispense with all these accoutrements, except the flowers which Tosca offers to the Holy Virgin. But, regrettably, they also dispense with the Sacristan's nervous tics, precisely indicated in the score where they have to occur; they serve to lend this comically fussy figure a touch of the grotesque.

The conductor of the first production was Leopoldo Mugnone, who had directed *La Bohème* at Palermo and gained for that opera its first great triumph. The producer was Tito Ricordi (1865–1932), the son of Puccini's publisher. Tito was one of the first in Italy to realize the growing importance of a carefully prepared *regia* and good acting in realistic opera, and *Tosca* offered him an excellent opportunity to show his gift for paying minute attention to scenic detail and working indefatigably with the cast, as he was to do again with *Madama Butterfly* and *La fanciulla del west*.[1] But Tito Ricordi committed a tactical error in bringing with him F. A. von Hohenstein, a famous stage designer of German descent, which was much resented in Roman circles. He also created a storm of protest when he gave strict instructions that no outsiders, including critics and relatives of the artists, were to be admitted to the rehearsals. What with Tito's dictatorial behaviour, and the rumour that Puccini's rivals[2] and their hangers-on were to be present in order to wreck the première whatever the artistic merits of the new work, compounded by the fact that Rome, being jealous of its standing as the country's capital, was not going to permit itself to be influenced by what northern cities like Milan and Turin thought of Puccini and his 'facile' successes, it was no wonder that the artists on that evening of 14 January felt as if they were sitting on a powder-keg likely to explode at any moment. (Some had even received anonymous letters threatening them with violence.) To add to first-night nerves, before the beginning of the performance a police officer had come to see Mugnone in his dressing-room in order to warn him that a bomb might be thrown into the auditorium, in which case the conductor was to strike up the National Anthem! Queen Margherita, members of the government and senators were to attend, and this lent substance to the rumour that a political assassination was being planned. Such rumours seemed to have something to do with the general political situation in Italy at the time. Since the termination of the unsuccessful war against Abyssinia in 1896, the country was rent by social unrest and discontent caused by worsening economic conditions. There had been riots in the North and South which the government of King Umberto I ruthlessly suppressed, and Parliament was dissolved by royal decree at the end of June 1899. There had already been two attempts on the king's life by anarchists, and indeed the king was assassinated at Monza in July 1900, six months after the première of *Tosca*. Against this larger background, the rumours surrounding this first night would naturally have been alarming.

The performance began with noisy disturbances in the auditorium, and Mugnone broke off and rushed backstage in fear and trepidation (years before, he had experienced a real bomb-throwing at the Liceo of Barcelona causing many deaths). Yet the cause of the uproar proved entirely harmless: some late-comers had tried to reach their seats which led to violent protests on the part of those already seated. Calm was restored, the opera was begun again, and remained undisturbed until the end. There is little doubt, however, that the extraordinarily tense atmosphere told on the quality of the performance. This came out in some press notices that spoke of 'first-night nerves and anxieties', and pointing out that successive performances would bring out details and values not perceived at the première. The most sensible and most comprehensive review was published by the critic of the *Corriere della Sera*, Alfredo Colombani, who declared that the main problem Puccini had had to face in *Tosca* was to 'adapt the music to naked facts and swift-changing incidents and to a fragmentary, rapid and agitated dialogue; in all', Colombani wrote, 'the composer has been wholly successful'. According to this critic, Puccini succeeded in ennobling an action which might otherwise have suggested the 'most reprehensible vulgarity'. Colombani considered the libretto an improvement on Sardou's play; from the purely musico-dramatic point of view he was right. Nevertheless, he felt that the opera still suffered from the 'defects of the original drama – psychological poverty and an excess of melodramatic situations which hindered Puccini in the free play of his imagination. This is perhaps the weak point of *Tosca*.' Indeed, the majority of the critics directed their shafts at the libretto rather than the music, finding it unsuited to Puccini's genius which appeared at moments to be 'suffocated' by it. The importance which the press attached to the new opera, which was certainly a great event in Italy's operatic life, may be gauged from the fact that the *Corriere d'Italia* devoted its entire front page to a discussion of it, offering the composer its congratulations on what he had achieved, yet deploring that he had attempted something 'the futility of which ought not to have escaped him'. So much for the reception by the press.

As for Puccini, he thought that *Tosca* was a near failure. But, as with *La Bohème*, he and the critics were proved wrong by the public, with whom the opera was an instant success. In the words of the old French tag, the audience showed more sense than Voltaire. Twenty more performances were given at the Costanzi before full houses, and in the same year the opera was produced at a large number of other Italian theatres, with La Scala (under Toscanini) coming immediately after Rome. *Tosca* reached Covent Garden on 12 July, only six months after the Rome production, where it was given in Italian with Milka Ternina in the title-role, Fernando De Lucia as Cavaradossi and Antonio Scotti as Scarpia, a part which this singer interpreted to perfection until his retirement in 1933. Between 1900 and the present day famous Toscas at Covent Garden have included Emmy Destinn, Maria Jeritza,[3] Rosa Raisa, Maria Caniglia, Margherita Grandi, Ljuba Welitsch, Maria Callas and Shirley Verrett. Eminent Cavaradossis at Covent Garden were Enrico Caruso, Benjamino Gigli, Giuseppe Di Stefano, Carlo Bergonzi, Luciano Pavarotti and Placido Domingo. Great Scarpias were, next to Scotti, Mariano Stabile, Lawrence Tibbett, Tito Gobbi, Gabriel Bacquier, Kostas Paskalis and Ingvar Wixell. A memorable *Tosca* production was that by Franco Zeffirelli on 21 January 1964, with Callas in the name-part and Gobbi as Scarpia.

Critical history

Of all Puccini's operas *Tosca* has had the most controversial critical history since its birth. The first Italian critics attacked it largely on account of its libretto, and almost the same may be said of the critical reception in other countries. Oddly enough, the majority of the English papers were not prepared to commit themselves one way or the other. Thus Herman Klein, music critic of the *Sunday Times*, wrote in his book, *The Golden Age of Opera*, largely about the high quality of the performance and the audience 'cheering themselves hoarse' on the occasion of the Covent Garden première.[4] Almost the only exception was *The Times* which came down wholly in favour of *Tosca*:

In his *Manon Lescaut* and again in *Bohème* the composer showed himself a master of the art of poignant expression, and it is most gratifying to find that

6 Act I. Tito Gobbi as Scarpia and Maria Callas as Tosca, Covent Garden, 1964

he can handle the larger passion of Tosca with as certain a touch as he displayed in treating the less strenuous grief of his two former heroines. Such scenes as the love-making of the first act, the horrible scene of the torture in the second, or the tragic dénouement of the whole are treated with wonderful skill and sustained power, so that each act rises to its natural climax and therefore makes a tremendous effect.

In marked contrast to this, the *New York Times* concluded its review of the first American production with 'Puccini will do better work with a better story'. The reception by the Parisian press was summed up by the critic of the *Mercure de France* – 'The opera is coarsely puerile, pretentious and vapid', while the *Neue Freie Presse* of Vienna spoke of 'psychological discrepancies and violent contrasts'. R. A. Streatfeild, in the fourth edition of *Grove*, declared *Tosca* 'a prolonged orgy of lust and crime made endurable by the beauty of the music'. The most eminent anti-Puccinian, past or present, was Gustav Mahler; given the spirituality and the high ethos of his artistic aspirations, this is not difficult to understand. *Tosca* seems to have been his special *bête noire*. In April 1903, conducting in Lvov (Lemberg) in Poland, Mahler visited the opera, where he saw *Tosca* for the first time. In a letter to his wife (20 April) he ridiculed it:

A most excellent production in every way. One is flabbergasted (*paff*) to find such a thing in an Austrian provincial town. But the work! In the first act a papal procession with continual clangour of bells (especially brought from Italy) – Act 2. A man is *tortured* with horrible cries, another stabbed with a pointed bread-knife – Act 3. A view over all Rome from a citadel and again mighty tintinnabulations from a fresh set of bells. A man shot by a firing-squad. I got up before the shooting and left. Needless to say, the work was another sham masterpiece (Meistermachwerk). Nowadays any cobbler orchestrates to perfection.[5]

During Mahler's tenure of the directorship of the Vienna Hofoper (1897–1907) *Tosca* was never produced there; its Austrian première took place at the Volksoper under Alexander von Zemlinsky in February 1907. *La Bohème* was given at the Hofoper in 1903, but was not conducted by Mahler. By the time that *Butterfly* was first performed at the Hofoper (October 1907) Mahler had resigned.

The next important Puccini-hater was the Italian musicologist, Fausto Torrefranca (1883–1955), who was the intellectual leader of an anti-operatic movement among the Italian avant-garde in the first decade of this century. In 1912 Torrefranca published a book with the significant title *Giacomo Puccini e l'opera internazionale* in which he tore the composer limb from limb. Puccini made no public reply, and his private correspondence contains only very vague allu-

sions to this painful interlude. Torrefranca started his attack from
the narrow and one-sided premise that the great tradition of Italian
music was to be found, not in opera, but in the instrumental music of
the seventeenth and eighteenth centuries. He went so far as to declare
that opera was a mongrel and did not reflect the native genius of
music. The rot, according to him, had set in with Monteverdi, while
Puccini illustrated 'all the decadence of present Italian music, all its
cynical commercialism, all its pious impotence and the triumph of
internationalism'. He says little about *Tosca*, but that little is damn-
ing enough.

Tosca might appear to be realistic, but it is not: even the excess of realism
(*verismo*) – and it is a realism crude and full of improbabilities which are not
so much of a practical and actual nature as of an ideal and sentimental order –
is a kind of romanticism. This is sublime in the sense that it lies outside the
sane and safe conscience of art.

Torrefranca then establishes two kinds of sublimity – the trivial and
the ideal. 'In *Tosca* there is only the first kind, namely rottenness: in
fact it is the only kind that Puccini, ignorant of the essence of romanticism, could understand.' Torrefranca concluded with the
prophecy that 'in a few decades hardly anything will be remembered
of Puccini's work'.[6] The book was written when its author was ap-
proaching his thirties, and in later years he regarded it as a 'necessary
sin of youth'; yet he claimed that what he had written forced Puccini
to re-examine his work and as a result his later operas were of a more
original character.

Behind Torrefranca's polemics was the strong conviction, shared
by all the young composers of the time, chief among them Pizzetti,
Malipiero and Casella – all three born in the early 1880s, a generation after Puccini – that native opera had run its course and had
become effete; and that a new *risorgimento*, a rejuvenation of Italian
music, could only be brought about by the assimilation of the spirit
and style of the great instrumental masters of the past – Frescobaldi,
Corelli, Veracini, Vivaldi and others.[7] The monopoly that opera
enjoyed in the musical life of Italy was deeply resented, vocalism
condemned, and the point was finally reached where the young fire-
brands clamoured for a ban on all composers who had devoted
themselves exclusively to opera. Mascagni retorted by saying that he
would write a symphony only when he felt his imagination to be
entirely exhausted. And there is Puccini's remark to his later librettist, Giuseppe Adami: 'If only I could be a symphonic writer! I should
then at least cheat time and my public.' By diverting creative energy

from opera to instrumental music the avant-garde hoped to bring about that '*ristabilimento dell'equilibrio*' they so much desired, and that was achieved in the large amount of purely instrumental music composed in Italy during the first half of this century. (This process had begun in the 1880s with such older composers as Martucci, Bossi, Sgambati and Sinigaglia.)

In contrast to Puccini, the new anti-operatic movement was both idealistic and nationalistic: idealistic because it wished to turn away from the *bourgeois* mentality of realist opera with its lack of spirituality and high moral values; nationalistic because it demanded an art exclusively nurtured in the old Italian soil and freed of the influences of both late German romanticism and French impressionism. In a thoughtful book which included a fairly balanced study of Puccini, Pizzetti reproached the entire impressionist school (notably Debussy) for its over-refinement, its growing exclusion of the life of the emotions, 'its prodigious faculty of stifling the will to live'; on the other hand, he accused Puccini and the other Italian realists of having sinned in the opposite direction by their emotional excesses and their superabundance of vitality, which, so ran Pizzetti's argument, defied full translation into satisfactory aesthetic expression.[8]

Not surprisingly, the extreme position occupied by the young iconoclasts of the 1900s was, in their maturity, gradually relinquished. Alfredo Casella (1883–1947), Gain Franceso Malipiero (1882–1973) and, especially, Ildebrando Pizzetti (1883–1968) began to turn their attention to the operatic stage, though guided by aesthetic and stylistic principles entirely different from those of Puccini. Pizzetti with his fifteen or so operas,[9] and Malipiero with some thirty to his name, may be said to have opened fresh paths for the post-Puccinian opera, but they are paths, not avenues. Pizzetti adhered to pervasive declamation in the voice part, and, for dramatic reasons reduced to a minimum the static lyrical element. Malipiero eliminated all dramatic dialectic and character development. Interesting though these innovations proved at the time their work did not have that universal appeal which Verdi, Puccini and others who stuck to the old '*melodramma*' of the nineteenth century still continue to command. Aesthetic theories that by-pass the natural laws of the musical theatre have little chance of leading to enduring results. It is a sobering comment on those high-minded reformers and on the present state of Italian opera that the only modern Italian whose operas have had an international audience happens to apply the much-derided Puccinian canons. This is Gian Carlo Menotti (b. 1911) who since

1928 has lived in America. Endowed with an extraordinary sense of the theatre, Menotti has an advantage over Puccini in being his own librettist, but on the level of originality and memorability of invention the comparison with the lucca master wholly ceases to be profitable.

The most influential of the later anti-Puccinians is Joseph Kerman, who has been Professor of Music at Oxford and at Berkeley, in California. In 1956 Kerman published a stimulating book, *Opera as Drama*, in which he mounted a scathing attack on Puccini and Strauss, whom he accused of 'a coarseness of sensitivity and a deep cynicism towards true dramatic values'.[10] Of all the Italian composer's works it was *Tosca* that aroused his severest indignation, on account of its 'café-music banality'[11] which led him to term the opera 'a shabby little shocker',[12] a phrase that has stuck to it ever since. Since it is important to provide the reader with the principal testimonies for and against, I quote an excerpt from Kerman's book:

Let us look at the last act [of *Tosca*]. The fact that it shows some similarities to the final act of *Otello* – and does not Scarpia invoke Iago in Act I? – should facilitate analysis.

Like Verdi, Puccini found himself beginning his last act with memories of great tension and violence, and with a situation conducive to an impressive hush before the catastrophe. With the 'Willow Song,' Verdi made this into an ominous hush which seems directed; as Puccini did not capture this quality, his scene seems rather to wait. He too employs a folk-song, sung off-stage by a Shepherd Boy as a misty, pink dawn is about to break. Presently a lengthy orchestral passage overloaded with Matin bells introduces the hero Cavaradossi, who converses briefly with the Gaoler; unlike the orchestral entrance of Otello, this is static, a single mood. Left alone, Cavaradossi recalls a rather warm dream of love in his famous aria '*E lucevan le stelle*.' Tosca enters with news of the 'reprieve,' and the score is heavy with leitmotives. As soldiers come, the action progresses swiftly to the final *coup de théâtre*. Tosca leaps off the parapet, and the orchestra concludes *tutta forza con grande slancio* with a repetition of the melody of '*E lucevan le stelle*.' The scheme is, again, superficially like that of *Otello*.

Now the first part of this act, up to the entrance of Tosca, is one of the most undramatic things in opera; *not* because nothing much happens on the stage, but because nothing happens in the music. It is indeed the penultimate demonstration of Puccini's insufficiency before the demands of Sardou's obvious melodrama. (The ultimate demonstration is the curiously passionless dialogue with Tosca that follows.) Possibly the Shepherd's song might have been integrated dramatically, but Puccini wished only to strike a mood of melancholy, which is inappropriate to Cavaradossi's position on its own, and doubly so when it leads into the attenuated bell-passage at his entrance, then into his mawkish aria. If Puccini had no more insight into or sympathy with the condemned hero's feelings at this crisis, he would have done better to leave them alone, as Verdi did with Manrico's at the end of *Il Trovatore*.

But patently Cavaradossi was not the primary concern. What mattered was not his plight, but the effect it could make on the audience. Puccini's faint emotionality is directed out over the footlights; he will let us have a good cry at Cavaradossi's expense. This at once makes for a complete extinction of the poor painter as a dramatic protagonist, and forms a shield against any serious feelings which Sardou, even, might have hoped to arouse in us.

As for the Shepherd's folk-song, it appears then to be as extraneous as the choirboys and the cardinal of Act I, an insertion not for any dramatic end, but for display of floating lyricism. This kind of thing is a weakness even with a composer of truer lyric talent. It is hardly necessary to contrast the parallel element in *Otello*, the 'Willow Song,' which not only makes Verdi's hush, but also wonderfully fills Desdemona's character and clarifies her fate. In the last act of *Otello*, the music for the hero's entrance, too, is crucially involved with the drama. Never once in four acts does Verdi interpolate pageantry or lyricism without a telling influence on the drama.

Tosca leaps, and the orchestra screams the first thing that comes into its head, '*E lucevan le stelle.*' How pointless this is, compared with the return of the music for the kiss at the analogous place in *Otello*, which makes Verdi's dramatic point with a consummate sense of dramatic form. How pointless, even compared with the parallel place in *La Bohème*, where Rudolfo's surge of pain does at least encompass the memory of Mimi's avowal. But *Tosca* is not about love; '*E lucevan le stelle*' is all about self-pity; Tosca herself never heard it; and the musical continuity is coarse and arbitrary. Once again, this loud little epilogue is for the audience, not for the play. What a shame (we are to feel), what a shame that butterflies are broken on this excellently oiled wheel. For they are, after all, still the fragile butterflies of the new Arcadia that is Puccini's Bohemia, flirting, fluttering, carefully fixing their crinolines in garrets. Cavaradossi is Marcello, with commission, but with no more sense of reality; Mimi is caricatured as La Tosca, with her simpering '*Non la sospiri la nostra casetta*' and her barcarole love-theme. But what had a certain adolescent charm in the earlier opera is preposterous here, with Spoletta, Sciarrone, Baron Scarpia, and the headscrew. I do not propose to analyze the musical texture of *Tosca*; it is consistently, throughout, of cafè-music banality. If Joyce Kilmer or Alfred Noyes had taken it into his head to do a grand poetic drama on Tosca, that would have been something analogous in the medium of language.

But it is scarcely believable that such a play would have held thae stage, or that it would be bracketed with Shakespeare, or that it would have become a favorite criterion for poetic drama. It would have its adherents, no doubt; and before those who would be impressed by the quality of the verse, one could only maintain discreet silence, as before those who are awed by Scarpia's chords or touched by the '*Vissi d'arte.*' The really insidious errors are three: first, the idea that Puccini's banality and Sardou's can somehow excuse one another and elevate each other into drama; second, that this is worth staging and buying season tickets to watch; and third, that this represents the true achievement of the art of opera.

The more fully one knows the real peaks of this achievement, the more clearly one sees the extent of Puccini's failure, or more correctly, the triviality of his attempt.[13]

Is one wrong in sensing here the puritanical streak of a New Englander? But like Torrefranca ('a necessary sin of youth'), Kerman, who wrote his book in his early thirties, seems to have mellowed in later years. When I asked him to contribute an anti-*Tosca* essay to this volume, Kerman declined, remarking that he did not have much more to say on the subject and would just as soon let old inflammations die down.

To enter into a polemic about the qualities of *Tosca* would be futile. It cannot be denied, however, that some people genuinely feel wholly out of sympathy with the world of Puccini's operas. They may object to his all-pervasive sensuality-cum-sentimentality. Puccini deliberately aims, especially in his middle-period works, at our tear-ducts: three of his four most celebrated operas are 'tear-jerkers'. There is also his undeniable streak of vulgarity – inevitable in full-blooded artists instinct with animal vitality, as witness the younger Verdi, Tchaikovsky, Strauss, Elgar, Balzac, Zola and Dickens. There is Puccini's calculated assault on our sensibilities and – perhaps most damaging in the eyes of the high-minded – the ethos, or rather lack of it, of his art. But we must not forget that for Italian (and French) opera composers the theatre is not a temple, not a moral institution, not the vehicle for *Weltanschauung*, metaphysics and 'deep' thought, but an arena in which large, heterogeneous audiences are brought together to be entertained and amused. Italian opera of the past two hundred years has always addressed itself to the majority and aimed at a broad appeal. Rossini, Donizetti, Verdi, Puccini and his contemporaries would have endorsed Defoe's proposition: 'If any man were to ask me what I suppose to be a perfect style of language I would answer, that in which a man speaking to 500 people, all of common and various composites, idiots and lunatics excepted, should be understood by them all and in the same sense in which the speaker intended to be understood.' They would have, no less readily, subscribed to Baudelaire's hyperbole: 'Any book that is not addressed to the majority – in numbers and intelligence – is a stupid book.'

Admittedly, Puccini does not set his sights very high. Yet, in saying this, do we not imply a moral judgement that seriously interferes with our aesthetic enjoyment? Works performed year in year out and genuinely loved and admired by the world at large must, it seems to me, possess *some* values, even if these offend against the taste of an élite. We may accuse an artist of holding views which as moral and spiritual tenets strike us as shallow or false. Yet we cannot withhold our admiration if he transmits his views into an art of such intensity of feeling, inner conviction and strength of imagination as to make them perennially interesting and persuasive. This is certainly the case with Puccini. As for *Tosca*, there is certainly an aspect to it that may offend the purist. But the opera was not written for him, or the aesthete or the man of perilously refined taste. It is a bold man who will assert that to relish lusty fullbloodedness in art is incompatible with aesthetic enjoyment – on the contrary, it may be a sign of a healthy, unwarped artistic instinct. Here is Baudelaire again: 'The autocrats in thought, the distributors of praise and blame, the monopolists of the things of the mind, have told you that you have no right to feel and enjoy – they are the Pharisees.'

7 *Interpretation: some reflections*

BY TITO GOBBI

I remember distinctly the first time Floria Tosca entered my life. It was years before I, as Baron Scarpia, was to take a hand in directing her tragic fate, but I can see her now in my mind's eye. I still hear the sweet impatience of her 'Mario! Mario!' sung off-stage. I still feel the *frisson* of excited expectancy which passed through the audience. And then she was there – entering the Church of Sant'Andrea della Valle with royal bearing, her left arm encircling her offering of flowers, extended so that the light caught the sheen on her sleeve and shoulder. She hardly touched the floor in the lightness of her tread – a marvellous vision, complete in its expression of art: La Divina Claudia Muzio.

Even then I think I sensed something of the elements which combined to make that perfect entry. Infinite research and study had prepared the groundwork, imagination had been brought to bear on the knowledge thus absorbed, and a tremendous flair for the projection of a unique personality had completed the miracle. Fascinated by the way in which singing and acting were blended in a harmonious whole, I dreamed that one day perhaps I would be able to do the same.

And so I fell in love with the work and have remained in love with it for the rest of my life – totally. I love the libretto – dramatic, strong and hard, yet rich in beautiful poetry. I love the music – melodic and descriptive, the inspiration for every facet of the drama and every reaction of an intelligent performer. (That magical walk of Muzio, for instance, was so completely right, following the rhythm of the triplets with which Puccini accompanies Tosca's theme.) I spare a slight smile of pity for those condescending critics who presume to look down on *Tosca* – perhaps because it is so easily accessible. But, after all, the loss is theirs. For me the great gain was the role of Scarpia, which has given me joy and the utmost artistic satisfaction, offering as it does almost limitless possibilities to exercise imagination and fantasy.

To attempt to outline and analyse the characters in *Tosca* would demand months of writing, always with the frustrating awareness that the end still remained beyond reach. But let me begin by setting down how I personally approached the role which I was called on to play 870 times in my career. It is the same approach which I have used for every part I have played, but even more arduous because of the strong opposition of reluctant producers and conductors who thought the strong role would 'ruin my . . . beautiful voice'.

As I have often said, in the many years of my singing career I went to the opera as spectator little more than 20 times. This does not mean that I dislike opera as a spectacle, but I have always been afraid of being influenced by the interpretations of other artists. I could not renounce the excitement of discovering *for myself* the character of the various personages, or lose the joy of inventing every night something new, living my role and not just playing it. Incidentally, therefore, I cannot judge my colleagues artistically, having known them very little from that point of view. Too bad, of course! For thus I deprived myself of the privilege of speaking badly of anyone.

This method however has enabled me to work without outside suggestions, compelling me to the most serious concentration, stimulating all the resources of my imagination, to the extent of splitting myself, as it were, so that I saw the product of my preparation – in this case Scarpia – standing in front of myself onstage or turning his back to me. I supported him and gave him courage, as I strove to make him always alive, important and present. I was able to control his voice, his breathing and his gestures. I took care of the position of his hands, of the significant movement of his cloak; I restrained his walking, so that he kept the right distance from the others. Was I the puppet-master of myself? I do not know. But I tried to feel and imagine myself as I wanted to appear to my audience.

When I say that I knew my characters from the back, I mean that literally. It never happened to me that a tape or a belt showed outside my coat, or the little tail of my wig was crooked, or the label of my costume-maker was visible on the collar of my cloak. I always built my interpretation with patience and real love, and I made myself up as Scarpia hundreds of times at home, between three mirrors so that I could see myself from every angle. I do exactly the same with each one of my characters. I studied with great care shoes and buckles, belts and swords, jewels – though these, little by little, I have stripped away. I have drawn and moulded my characters, literally, so that I can see them physically, and this has been a great pleasure and amusement which has occupied many, many hours of my life. Not as a hobby but as a real and deep interest, stemming from my great love and respect for the job and my unshakable sense of artistic duty and responsibility.

But I would not have it thought that I regard Scarpia (or any other character I have played) as someone in isolation, someone who taken on life only as he comes on to the stage. What is the panorama of the period and place in which he lives? What are the elements which make up the world from which he comes to play out his few dramatic hours before the public? If all this is not in the back of my mind, how can I behave, move, react as the *whole* Scarpia should? And this is where the preliminary study and the welding of fact and fancy come in.

I do not ask anxiously what is historically true and what is literary fiction in the story and characters of an opera (though I make it my business to be informed about this). Too academic an approach in this respect is not important for a full realization of the character conceived by composer and librettist. But as I made my eager researches I began to blend the elements which make up the back-cloth, as it were, to the drama: Naples, the Bourbons, Sicily, Napoleonic France – all are involved. Then there is Queen Caroline (the sister of Marie Antoinette), unseen on the stage but referred to several times as a living, important element in the strands of the story. Did she have an affair with Scarpia? I am inclined to think she did. At any rate, he was a protégé of hers, a Sicilian, strong, elegant, with compelling glance, and a suggestion of the colours and perfumes of the South about him.

Then the young Cavaradossi, the painter, a pupil of David, come from Paris to Rome, where he has been caught up in Italy's revolutionary movements, based on the first republics of Naples and Rome. Somewhere in the background passes the figure of Lady Hamilton. Lord Nelson is a person undoubtedly known to all these people. The Pope is in exile. We have the battle of Marengo . . . and so on. I build with all these elements a very 'logical' mosaic and make it mine. I strongly believe in it, just as Scarpia did – if he really existed. He is for me a most fascinating character, still alive today, though I no longer impersonate him.

For years, seeking the right approach and presentation, I practised my (his) way of walking, the characteristic swing of the cloak, the *rhythm* (always listening to the magical way Puccini indicates this). And a thousand times I tried my voice in a thousand colours and inflexions. I tormented myself, my wife and various conductors with my anxiety to find the immediate direct impact of his first appearance onstage, to the sound of those fateful chords. Arrogant, tremendous, confident and terrible, yet with outward composure, refined and inflexible. A man before whom indeed 'all Rome trembled'. How did one convey that instantaneously? Then one day, during an unsatisfactory rehearsal, I suddenly sang words and music without anything of personal interpretation added – and all at once the great effect was there! Puccini had already thought of everything, I discovered. All I had to do was be faithful and humble.

It is enough for Scarpia to stand there, the glint in his eye sufficient to disperse the people. A refined man, possibly slightly overplaying the aristocrat, with no need to shout or lash about to assert his authority. Thus I gave free range to my flair, if that is the word, for interpretation. I mean the instinct for translating into terms of the theatre the inner knowledge of the character already acquired and freely woven by my fantasy and imagination – *though always respectfully close to the score*. There was infinite pleasure and satisfaction in giving the correct degree of light and shade to every word and expression, so that my action 'requested' the reactions I wanted in others.

I have always painted with my imagination while singing, giving to the sound various colours and intensities. The voice changes when you tell something happy or sad. There are warm and cold colours that one should use accordingly. I have enjoyed using the splendid palette with all shades, sometimes in sharp contrast or faded like water-colours. After all, what is a voice? Nothing in itself, just air passing through two tiny cords. But through mind and heart it becomes the *art* of expressing all human feelings. To colour the voice means to clothe the words or phrases with expression that very often suggests colours.

Sometimes I would suggest to my colleagues the reaction which I had in mind, and if I succeeded in convincing them it was because I myself was totally convinced. The reality of this co-operation occasionally had unexpected results. One illustrious colleague refused for years to perform Tosca with me because she could not overcome the indignation and revulsion which I, as Scarpia, aroused in her. Finally I persuaded her; we studied the opera together, and I took charge of the production, the better to be a support to her. The first night arrived and everything went smoothly until the death of Scarpia – 'È morto . . . or gli perdono . . .' ('He is dead . . . now I pardon him . . .')

Then suddenly, as she saw the *open eyes* of the dead man, she gave me a look of utter horror and, trembling and screaming, she ran from the stage, leaving me alone and in agony, without candles or crucifix, still and helpless before a stupefied audience, which was stunned by this totally unfamiliar finale to Act II.

So much for my personal interpretation of Scarpia, the individual character. But as time went on I felt so enriched by my knowledge of the work that I thought I must pass on some of this accumulated experience, and so I came to production and teaching – the most wonderful widening of my artistic horizons. It was like entering for the first time a marvellous great hall of the palace in which I used to live. I discovered new beauties and new riches. I also learned to listen to someone else's ideas and questions before stating mine. I learned to pursue what I had hitherto only dimly perceived or imagined. I learned that there is no limit to knowledge and that the more you know the more you want to know. I discovered an endless source of energy which kept alive the joy in my own work and the companion joy of sharing this generously with others.

Puccini, as I have said, was one of the great men of the theatre, and his operas are conceived and carefully calculated for stage presentation. Nevertheless, there is still room for the producer to spread the wings of his own ideas within the framework constructed by librettist and composer.

In *Tosca* I believe that Scarpia is the key character. Not because he was 'my' character, but because it is he who drives the action with almost demonic energy and expertise. In my production I build everything around him – this terrifying but controlled, elegant creature. And because he is controlled, the rest of the cast must resist all temptation to overplay their parts or degenerate into uncontrolled melodramatic excess.

He is very much aware of his position as Roman Chief of Police, making a central figure of himself whenever he has a chance to do so. He should never be the stereotyped villain, but cold and authoritative, examining and enquiring, though with Tosca herself ceremonious, almost mellifluous. There are momentary changes in his attitude to Tosca, always led and dictated by the wonderfully subtle music which Puccini has given him. For instance, two startling bars in the first act are sufficient to prompt his impulsive move towards Tosca, instantly succeeded by a return to his usual suave manner as he offers her the holy water, marked by the sound of the bells. There is a touch of reproach in his voice at this moment, as though reproving her for the fact that she did not cross herself on entering the church, as a pious woman should.

He gives the impression of being scandalized when he shows her the Attavanti fan, with a sharp note on the phrase 'È arnese di pittore questo?', awakening her jealousy. Then, when the insinuating 'Qualcuno venne certo a sturbar gli amanti' provokes her to fury, he immediately reverts to apparently grave reproach, with his exclamation, 'In chiesa'. It is all there in the music. When he leads her to the door he clearly makes an advance, caressing her arm. But the moment she has gone he is once more the inflexible Chief of Police as he orders his henchmen to follow the jealous Tosca who will, 'like a good falcon', all unknowing lead them to the prey.

Musing on his position of power, he allows himself some moments of excited dreaming, in which he sees himself encompassing the death of Mario and his own possession of Tosca . . . The *Te Deum* arouses him and he comes back to reality, kneeling spectacularly and beating his breast, so that all may see him.

Act II opens with Scarpia sitting alone, the descending octaves suggesting, with their repetition, his wandering thoughts. But when he gets up and walks, the heavy chords indicate that we are indeed in the presence of the Chief of Police in his most official mood. The most dramatically telling effect, however, comes with the outburst of passion on 'Quest'ora io l'attendea . . .' ('This is the hour I've been waiting for . . .'). One of Puccini's most tremendous moments. Preceded by the recitative which mounts to splendid high notes for the baritone range, there come the long, ascending (and fiendishly difficult) phrases which truly depict the upsurge of passion.

The setting is Scarpia's room in the Palazzo Farnese. I choose to make it a beautiful studio, the walls covered with Roman landscapes painted by Vanvitelli. A butler attends the Baron, who sits at a very rich dining table – lace cloth, fine silver and crystal, precious china. All the furniture must be in a style previous to 1800, for the battle of Marengo (spoken of as taking place in the immediate present) took place on 14 June 1800. It must also be remembered that Pope Pius VI is a prisoner of Napoleon, so that French influence is not officially accepted in Rome but, thanks to a fine old tradition, very good taste in fashion and art prevails there.

And now to the glorious Floria Tosca herself. Was she born in the Veneto? I think she was – partly because, having been born there myself, I would like her to come from there! She is beautiful, like a Paolo Veronese portrait. She was born poor and brought up in a convent; but because of her gifts she became the pupil and protégée of great masters, eventually attaining the position of Prima Donna Assoluta in Rome and singing at the Court. She is madly in love with Mario Cavaradossi but, completely absorbed in her own happy life, she is not wildly excited about his painting – any more than he is about her singing. She accepts this without rancour. 'Stasera canto', she tells him, but adds reassuringly, 'ma è spettacolo breve' ('Tonight I sing – but it is a short performance').

The music of the love duet depicts her conflicting feelings of love and jealousy, but her almost naive indifference to his art shows when she asks, 'Chi è quella donna bionda lassù?' ('Who is the fair-haired woman up there?') The painting could hardly have been done during the morning or during the little time she leaves between one visit and the next, so it had obviously escaped her notice yesterday or the day before.

Mario lies easily, 'La vidi *ieri* ma fu puro caso . . . Non visto la ritrassi . . .' ('I saw her *yesterday* and I painted her unseen . . .'). It is the Sacristan who notices everything, who mutters knowledgeably, 'Di quella ignota che í *di passati* . . .' ('The unknown woman who in the *last few days* . . .').

But Tosca goes through life thoughtlessly happy with her love and her success, with rapidly changing emotions and thoughts, from quick jealousy to charming romanticism. The music helps her to describe in the love duet moonlight nights on the Appian Way and she almost competes with her lover in painting the beauties of nature, the hum of the insects, the awakening of the 'Agro Romano', ending with an irresistible 'Fiorite, o campi immensi', which completely carries Cavaradossi away, so that momentarily he even forgets his anxiety about Angelotti.

I don't think Tosca is violently or vulgarly jealous. Her doubts and objections are just passing clouds – 'Nuvole leggere, nuvole leggere . . . ' Theirs is a happy love, one of joy and romantic sensations which pass over and scarcely touch earthly hindrances.

In Act II, incredulous and surprised, they gallantly face the dramatic truth of facts previously ignored by them, and prepare to fight for justice against tyranny and infamy. In a sense the act develops into a great duel between Tosca and Scarpia, which can achieve supreme effects if the partners understand each other. Tosca becomes more and more nervous, and Scarpia more dangerous, contriving to show a pleasant exterior, a sort of false bonhomie, to give partial cover to the cruel, sadistic, sensual – and very vain – man.

7   Act II. Marie Collier as Tosca and Tito Gobbi as Scarpia, BBC 1, 1965

In her aria 'Vissi d'arte' Tosca weeps in bewildered self-pity, asking God why she is rewarded with such torment when she has always tried to do good and gave her jewels and her singing to the Madonna: a typical attitude from one with a rather innocently lightweight nature. Gathering strength, she fights desperately, throwing herself at Scarpia's feet, imploring him to save Mario. Then at the news of Angelotti's suicide and the last threat of Scarpia she gives in and calmly agrees to pay with her body for a passport for herself and Mario, firmly believing that will ensure their freedom.

While Scarpia writes, her distracted gaze perceives the knife. Momentarily she thinks of using it but rejects the idea. Then, when Scarpia excitedly rushes upon her with 'Tosca finalmente mia' she seizes the knife in a desperate attempt to defend herself and stabs him to death.

The movement is instinctive. She is not a woman to plan a murder or exult in carrying it out. On one occasion which I recall with some pleasure, an energetic soprano insisted that I let her stab me three times, and nothing would change her mind. During the performance, at 'Questo è il bacio di Tosca', she came to give me the second stab. I staggered to my feet with both arms extended and a most ferocious expression on my face – and had her running away with a heartfelt scream of terror, to hide in the farthest corner of the stage. She dropped the knife and I dropped dead on my back – in peace.

In Act III the less the scene is 'produced' the better it is. The dawn unveiling note by note, bar by bar, discloses the dome of St Peter's and the high roofs of the city. The act opens with the exquisite chiming of the church bells all over Rome. They follow each other, almost chase each other across the sky, announcing the dawn. The singing of the little shepherd recalls the magnificent prints by Pinelli and Piranesi. The Eternal City wakes, unaware that a new execution is about to stain the walls of the Castel Sant'Angelo with blood. The music suggests a moment of meditation, not to be interrupted by excessive manoeuvring of Austrian platoons changing guard. Certainly the castle cannot be empty, but it is best to have the minimum of action and listen to the music.

Following the miraculous tenor aria, which should unfold like a freshly discovered flower even though everyone in the audience knows it well, Floria arrives, believing wholly in her safe conduct. There is wonderful nervous excitement in the music depicting her entry, culminating in the great sonorous chord which marks their embrace, and followed by the long melodic phrases of their last duet.

Unlike Floria, Cavaradossi knows that Scarpia never yields, though he pretends to believe in order to delay the pain for Tosca. He strongly controls his emotion when he asks to hear her sweet voice again, knowing it will be for the last time, and his 'Parlami ancora come dianzi parlavi . . .' has a desperate accent, and silently he listens to her dreaming of escape over the sea.

Tosca, in her blind hope, brings a breath of life and confidence. Almost hysterically she evokes the killing of Scarpia, 'Io quella lama gli piantai nel cor . . . ' (a phrase that is the terror of all sopranos with its high C), and suddenly yields her hands to Mario's kisses and caresses: 'O dolci mani . . .' The tender melody encourages her to dream of their escape across the sea; she almost sees the boat sailing towards the light clouds ('Nuvole leggere'). She hopes with such certainty that she is even able to make a joke about what she believes to be the mock execution. She tells Mario how to fall convincingly, knowing about this from her own stage experience. Perhaps 'un po' per celia e un po'per non morir . . .' Like Butterfly's, her faith is blind and moving.

Like a Funeral March, the music brings in the execution squad. The farce in which she believes becomes the tragedy with which she cannot live. When she realizes that Mario is dead she weeps for herself, 'Povera la tua Tosca', calls Scarpia to judgement before God and throws herself from the battlements of Castel Sant'Angelo.

(It is a tremendous moment, but one in which every movement must be carefully rehearsed and understood. On one occasion a foreign producer for some reason had no time to explain the action to the platoon of soldiers. At the very last moment he tried with much gesturing to convey to them that they had to rush to the wall and look down where Tosca had fallen. Willing but confused, they thought they had got the message and, one after another, they all jumped over after her.)

As in all fine works of the theatre, the minor roles are often the structure which support the drama, and an acute interpreter can find new and interesting aspects, while remaining within the limits of his or her role. Thus, from the first moment of curtain-rise I have Angelotti stumble over a kneeling stool as he enters the darkened church, the music clearly indicating the piteous exhaustion with which he staggers in. I also have him hide in a confessional box as the Sacristan arrives before he can unlock the chapel, in this way heightening the terror of discovery to the last point of anguish. The Sacristan is not in my view a buffoon, and has no need to play for

8 Act II. Janis Martin as Tosca and Tito Gobbi as Scarpia, Lyric Opera of Chicago, 1971

cheap laughs. He is just a greedy grumbler, a witty tattler, dragging around the big church in his simple faith, limping slightly on his chatty and elegant music, complaining to the Madonna about the artist's dirty brushes, remarking on everything, and acting as a valuable foil to Cavaradossi, Tosca and Scarpia. In my production I use him a lot, and even have him guide the choir in the big procession. To him is entrusted one of the most serene and mystical moments, when he performs the exquisite *Angelus Domini*. I refuse to have him disturbed until the end, for too often the beautiful moment is drowned by the triumphant entry of the tenor, complete with noisy acclaim from the paid claque. A great mistake: for to put personal notice before anything else is to set the stamp of mediocrity upon oneself. The lesson of Hamlet to the Players is still valid, and a little modesty is always a good idea.

Even the six or eight 'sbirri' (henchmen) who precede and follow the entrance of Scarpia in the first act have their individual parts to play. They must immediately have the church under control, but 'senza dar sospetti' ('without arousing suspicion') and with the minimum of action. And I would like – no, I insist! – that the *sbirri* should have eyes only for him, ready to interpret and obey his smallest hint of command. Of course, for the producer the great treat is the procession which closes the first act: the assembling of the people in the church following the procession, with the Cardinal and all the appurtenances for the *Te Deum*. With candlesticks, incense, canopy and choir, I have them beautifully circling around the big pillars until they finally reach the nave, facing the audience when they sing.

It is all part of the glorious experience of serving the work with heart and brain and spirit. A sensitive artist faces every night the challenge of the various changes which can occur in a performance. He forgets his own identity and experiences an unparalleled pleasure in feeling and expressing new facets of that precious diamond – the human brain. That is why I would like all opera singers to remember that it is less important to earn astronomical fees than to be a worthwhile artist. And on a purely practical note, I would like them to ask for more piano rehearsals, the better to blend their interpretations and make the individual quality of each performer more vivid. Perhaps then conductors would follow with more care, love and (why not say it?) honesty, the music and the singers on stage.

I have had the privilege of performing Scarpia with the greatest prima donnas of my time and keep an endearing souvenir of them all. They were all magnificent in their different characterizations which was a challenge to me, as each of them had different reactions to my actions. The fiery Zinka Milanov, who generously left me alone in front of the curtain at my début at the Metropolitan Opera House; the dramatic Gina Cigna; Marie Collier, a real tiger whom I had to calm down before entering the scene; Renata Tebaldi, aloof and disdainful with her golden voice; and Maria Callas. I had the extraordinary privilege to bring back to the stage Tebaldi and Callas after a long absence. With Maria it was not playing but living; we were Tosca and Scarpia and felt completely free on stage on the strength of a perfect understanding. When the great duel of Act II ended we would first bow to each other in front of the curtain, like two gallant opponents, and then to the audience.

What else would I like, in listing my ideal 'conditions'? As I have said, I would like Mario to give the Sacristan time to finish his beautiful *Angelus*, and also not to distract our attention with anxious glances towards the chapel while Tosca is praying. We already know Angelotti is hiding there. He need not keep reminding us of the fact. I should also like it to be remembered that in a church – and in 1800 at that – one does not indulge in exaggerated displays of physical love, with uncontrolled embraces and sexual impulses better reserved for other places.

I should like Angelotti on his first appearance to listen to the music which guides him, and not just utter cavernous sounds which are absurd in any case in anyone physically so extremely weak. I should like the Sacristan to control that famous 'tic' of his and not to invite the audience to laugh their heads off. And I would personally appreciate it very much if he too would show terror at the entrance of Scarpia.

To everyone I would make a special plea for them to have it clear in their own minds that each role has its own dimension, suggesting when to come into the light and when to disappear. Action and reaction are very important so long as they last for the correct length of time, without obscuring one another. And I hope never again to see someone on the stage moving his lips as he follows the singing of a colleague.

I would like Floria Tosca to salute Scarpia with a polite, if cool, nod when he offers the holy water, instead of a startled turn of the head as though a toad has appeared beside her. And I wish to God that the *Te Deum* might be allowed to end without an overwhelming clamour of cannon, bells and bawling voices all competing madly against the orchestra.

I would like Scarpia to be hardly able to conceal his nervousness and anxiety while waiting for news at the beginning of Act II. He has not changed his costume, he is not going to the Cantata. He has other things to think about, knowing only too well that if he does not find Angelotti it may be his own head that will fall. I would like the 'Chief of Police' to use a manifestly different tone of voice and attitude towards the varying characters. Sometimes the refined gentleman has an outburst of rage, immediately controlled by his complex nature of bigot, satyr, sadist, courtier and hangman. He enjoys showing his different aspects, exalted and inebriated by wine and blood. The dangerous crescendo will at last overwhelm him, so that he falls to the knife of a fragile woman.

There are so many things still that I would like to list, solely for the purpose of doing better. Because even if I myself no longer sing Baron Vitellio Scarpia, he is still alive and fascinating and will go on long after me . . . as I willingly hand him over to my respected colleagues prepared to cope with him.

8 *Style and technique*

Tosca is, strictly speaking, not a music-drama in the accepted (Wagnerian) sense, but rather the early herald of the modern music-theatre, that is, a drama with a powerful, action-packed plot round which the music coils and recoils with snake-like suppleness and pliancy. Were it not for the lyrical episodes in which Puccini the musician asserts himself against Puccini the dramatist, the music might be defined as a function, or extension in sound, of the action. Nowadays when *Salome* and *Elektra* form part of the ordinary repertory, and when *Wozzeck* and, latterly, the three-act *Lulu* have come into their own – all these operas partake of the nature of music-theatre – it is difficult to realize the daring novelty that *Tosca* represented in the early 1900s. On the face of it, the subject seemed to defy operatic treatment, and it is a measure of Puccini's stature as a musical dramatist that he not only overcame its apparent unsuitability for musicalization but found valid musical equivalents for such scenes as Cavaradossi's torture and Scarpia's sexual frenzy. Sardou's play has vanished into limbo while Puccini's opera has been proclaiming its extraordinary vitality in countless productions over more than eight decades. Moreover, *Tosca* provides an outstanding example, like the large majority of successful operas, of the composer's acute instinctive awareness of the inner and, largely, imponderable laws that govern action and music as expressed in the right balance between the dramatic (action-music) and the lyrical (aria, duet). At the root of Puccini's view of dramatic composition lay the dialectic that however powerful and forward-driving the action, opera must not be all movement and conflict but must have moments of stasis and repose when a character is enabled to reflect on himself and on his relationship to other characters, and project his thoughts and emotions in lyrical song.

As I said in the chapter on the genesis of the opera, *Tosca* was Puccini's first major attempt to break away from the sentimental

91

tragédie larmoyante of his two preceding operas and press forward in the direction of something stronger and harder of emotional fibre, something larger-than-life and with a touch of the heroic. It was a style that was to lead him via *La fanciulla del west* and *Il tabarro* to its consummation in *Turandot*, in which Scarpia is, as it were, transmogrified into the cruel Chinese princess while the heroic counterpart to Cavaradossi is represented by Calaf. (The parallels between the two operas extend also to the classical unities – the action of *Turandot* taking place within the space of twelve hours – to the removal of historical allusions and the presence of a motto theme.) The intimate miniatures of *Manon Lescaut* and, notably, *Bohème* are signally reduced in *Tosca* to make room for broad brush-strokes, and a new trenchancy informs the themes and motifs, especially those of Scarpia. Indeed, Puccini's characterization of the world of Scarpia and that of the lovers – evil versus good – is reminiscent of the two spheres that are pitted against each other in Weber's *Freischütz*, Wagner's *Lohengrin* and *Parsifal*,[1] an opera greatly admired by Puccini; it may well be that the served him as a model for his own projection of the confrontation of the two worlds in *Tosca*. But there is a fundamental difference: while the German work ends with good triumphing over evil, the Italian opera presents a nihilistic solution of the conflict – both worlds are destroyed.

Scarpia was Puccini's first major role for a baritone, in which he followed a time-honoured and psychologically well-founded tradition of opera according to which the villain's part was almost invariably reserved for a low male voice. He thus extended his previous scheme which was based on soprano–tenor as his main voice categories. Scarpia is by far the most complex and therefore most interesting of the opera's three main characters. But it is debatable whether Puccini did full musical justice to his villain as did Wagner to Klingsor and Verdi to Iago. His liabilities are his three monologues, which in my opinion lack that touch of the demonic or the diabolical manifest in Klingsor and Iago. The absence of a broadly sustained cantabile in his music is deliberate – a Scarpia cannot indulge in the quasi *bel canto* style of Tosca and Cavaradossi. Take for example his second-act aria, 'Ha più forte sapore'. True, it opens with something like a cantilena (Ex. 4g) rising in stepwise (diatonic) progressions and with a regular, balanced phrase-structure, but all this is soon destroyed by hectic outbursts in wide intervals and irregular phrasing, with the shape of the vocal line primarily dictated by the words. This is typical of Scarpia's set-pieces and serves as a characterizing element, in marked contrast with the arias of the lovers. Where Puccini scores is in Scarpia's action-music which is terse, pithy and, above all, *farouche* and in which we note a high level of dissonance combined with chromatic writing. An entirely new feature of this part is the widespread use of the whole-tone scale which Puccini had used years before Debussy's *Pelléas et Mélisande* (1902): once in the orchestral prelude to Act III of *Manon Lescaut* (1893) and again in Act IV of *Bohème* where a certain chord progression (Ex. 24a) is almost identical with that of the 'Scarpia' motto (Ex. 1a). Yet, while in these two operas no extra-musical symbol seems to be attached to the whole-tone scale, in *Tosca* Puccini, following in the footsteps of certain Russian composers,[2] makes this scale the musical equivalent of the evil and sinister in Scarpia; and this gives the music of the character a more advanced, more modern element than is the case with music of the lovers. All the motifs closely associated with this character, such as the 'Scarpia' motto, its extension into the 'Well' motif and the 'Reflection' motif, are based on the whole-tone scale:

Ex. 1a 'Scarpia' motto

Ex. 1b 'Well' motif

Ex. 1c 'Reflection' motif

A notable feature of this scale is that it encapsulates the augmented fourth or tritone – the *diabolus in musica* of the medieval theorists, so called because it is so difficult for the singer to pitch this dissonant interval correctly. The augmented fourth forms the bass of Ex. 1a, and Puccini associates this interval[3] with 'negative' emotions – mental torment, fear and anxiety – as may seen from the chain of tritones at Angelotti's entrance:

Ex. 2b 'Angelotti' motif

Let me consider Scarpia's leitmotif (Ex. 1a) in greater detail. It is essentially a harmonic (non-melodic) idea similar to the chord of the diminished seventh used by Weber to symbolize the dark forces of Samiel (Satan) in *Der Freischütz*. Together with the 'Love' motif (Ex. 4e) it is the most frequently used in the opera. Puccini places it (as he does the 'Turandot' motif in the 'Chinese' opera) as a motto at the head of *Tosca*, when it is sounded before the rise of the curtain. It represents what the composer called 'il motivo di prima intenzione', and except for transpositions to other degrees of the whole-tone scale and rhythmic and instrumental changes, it undergoes, with one or two exceptions, no harmonic or intervallic alterations. The rigidity of this treatment, already seen in the 'steely' progression of three tonally unrelated major triads (B flat, A flat and E) in the motif itself, is intentional, and designed to denote the immutable evil and cruelty of Scarpia.

Two other means by which Puccini characterizes this figure are the orchestration and the dynamics. The dynamics, reflecting his brutal violence, include an extreme sound level (*ff*, *fff*, *sfz*) and markings such as *con tutta forza*, *con violenza* and *ruvido* (roughly). The orchestration favours in the tutti massed brass and percussion, and in the intimate quasi chamber-music passages, lower strings and woodwind. Indeed, characterization by means of a certain instrument or instruments is also heard in the music of the lovers. Prominent in Tosca's portrayal are the upper strings, the brighter woodwind (flute, oboe and clarinet) and harp, while Cavaradossi is associated with warm, mellow-sounding instruments like clarinet, horn and cello. There is a sad beauty in the four solo cellos preceding

Cavaradossi's 'E lucevan le stelle'. But these remarks can only indicate general tendencies in the orchestration, for Puccini mixes the variegated colours of his instrumental palette with great freedom and imagination.

Scarpia being the main vehicle for Puccini's verismo, it follows that in all the scenes with their persecutor his two victims are also affected by this style, notably in Act II. On the other hand, in their love scenes (Acts I and III), the contrast between their soaring lyricism and Scarpia's utterances is most marked, as witness the sustained cantabile, the regular phrase-structures and the firm, well-defined tonalities of the arias and duets. Moreover, these set-pieces are in 'closed' form (binary and ternary), vaguely parallelled in Scarpia's open-ended monologues. The only exception is the phrase-structure of Cavaradossi's lament in Act III – a verismo aria *par excellence*. These lyrical enclaves are like islands in the rapid current of the action.

Yet, notwithstanding these differences, there is a common denominator in the melodies of the opera that allows one to speak of a specific *Tosca* style. This is a design which shows, to a far greater degree than in other Puccini operas, a definite mould or pattern, namely a stepwise (diatonic) rise and/or fall of scale segments which more often than not alternate with wide intervals such as the fourth, fifth and, more rarely, the sixth. Ex. 4 contains a list of themes and motifs showing this characteristic fingerprint.

Ex. 4a 'Cavaradossi' theme

Ex. 4b Tosca's 'entrance' theme

Ex. 4c Tosca's arietta 'Non la sospiri'

Ex. 4d Cavaradossi's 'Love' motif: arietta 'Qual occhio al mondo'

Ex. 4e 'Love' motif

Ex. 4f Finale of Act I (Ecclesiatical theme)

Ex. 4g Scarpia's aria 'Ha più forte sapore'

Ex. 4h Scarpia's monologue 'Già mi struggea l'amor'

Ex. 4i 'Torture' motif

Ex. 4j From the prelude to Act III

Ex. 4k 'Trionfal di nuova speme'

The striking feature here is the diatonic nature of the examples; this, combined with a circular triplet movement or a rising opening, is in my opinion responsible for the sense of strength emanating from the score. Without wishing to press the point it seems to me that they have all sprung from the same matrix in Puccini's mind, or, to put it less abstractly, they are like branches of the same tree. Among the eleven examples I single out 4a and 4e because they show how the composer, by a careful distribution of scale segments and wide intervals, arrives at a melody of remarkable balance and shapeliness. Ex. 4e is one of the great themes of the opera.

Another characteristic of the melodic style is Puccini's predilection for *gruppetto*-like figures either for a decorative purpose (Ex. 5a) or in the service of expression (Ex. 5b, see also Exx. 9b, 15 and 18):

Ex. 5a Cadential figure

Ex. 5b

l'in - na - mo - ra - ta   To - sca è pri - gio - nie - ra____

Our next concern is with Puccini's technique for achieving continuity and coherence in *Tosca*. Like all post-Wagnerian composers he employs the orchestra as the means of obtaining a continuum, although the old 'number' scheme peeps through in the set-pieces which are mostly self-contained, separated as they are from the action-music by general pauses and double bars. Mention of the orchestra of course brings up the question whether Puccini's treatment of it can really be called symphonic. In the German sense, 'symphonic' means development and extensive variation of a given thematic idea. Now, there are 50 to 60 different themes and motifs in *Tosca*, yet none shows development in the German sense; at best it is spun out for a few bars but is mostly transposed in an unaltered stereotyped form to other keys.[4] Once or twice Puccini resorts to a contrapuntal combination of two ideas, as in Ex. 7 in which the 'Scarpia' motto is set against the Sacristan's distorted motif (interval-

Ex. 7

lic and rhythmic changes) to suggest the effect the Chief of Police has
on the timid cleric. A similar combination occurs at the opening of
Act II, where Angelotti's 'escape' theme is joined by the 'Love' motif
and followed by Cavaradossi's own 'Love' figure to reveal the direction that Scarpia's unspoken thought is taking (Ex. 8). In this last

Ex. 8

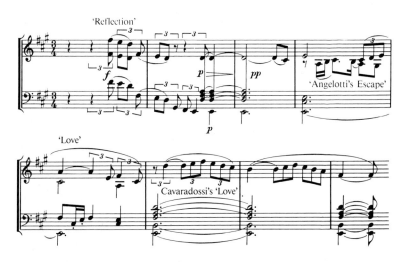

example the leitmotifs are used in a psychologically revealing sense,
as happened quite often with Puccini.

This brings us to a discussion of the composer's leitmotif as such,
and the treatment of it. As a rule his characterizing motifs are clear-
cut and suggestive, as for instance the 'Scarpia' motto, Tosca's
'Entrance' (Ex. 4b) and the 'Love' theme (Ex. 4e). Yet his handling of
the motifs, compared with that of Wagner and Strauss, differs in two
important respects. One is that Puccini does not use motifs with

strict consistency,[5] and the other is that very few undergo melodic-rhythmic alterations no matter how greatly the emotional or dramatic situation has changed after the motif's initial occurrence. Puccini's leitmotif looks back to the old pre-Wagnerian 'reminiscence' and is scarcely more than a label (Wagner's 'visiting-card') attached to a character or an object. Moreover, of the two functions which the leitmotif has fulfilled since Wagner – one dramatic and the other symphonic – Puccini's serves very largely the former. He does not weave his motifs into a continuous symphonic web, but simply juxtaposes them, in mosaic-like fashion, unaltered and merely transposed to another key. From the point of view of German music-drama, Puccini's technique may appear regressive, even primitive. Yet it would be wrong to chalk this up against a composer who, in the tradition of nineteenth-century Italian opera, perceived the singers as his chief dramatic agents, to whom the orchestra, for all its importance as the generator of mood and atmosphere, remains essentially subservient. Nevertheless, the Puccinian leitmotif does succeed in establishing a grid or framework of thematic references, thus contributing to musico-dramatic coherence.

Coherence is also achieved by means of the classical key-relationships and the more modern 'progressive' tonality. If we disregard the key sequences within an act and consider only its ending, we find in *Tosca* the following scheme: E flat major (Act I) – E minor (Act II) – E flat minor (Act III). (In *Bohème* there is a similar shift from the C major of Act I to C sharp minor in Act IV.) Unlike the movements of a symphony, the individual acts of *Tosca* do not centre in a definite key – they do not have a 'home-key'. However, broadly speaking, Act I favours the flat keys, the exception being the E major of the love scene which will be discussed later (p. 105); the A major of the choristers; and the Sacristan's *ballabile* which is, perhaps significantly, in the neutral key of C major denoting the banal, everyday nature of this character (compare the long-held C major chord in Act I, scene 2 of *Wozzeck* which symbolizes the common-place nature of the money the Soldier hands over to Marie). In Puccini's Act II, flat keys in major and minor predominate, though the 'Murder' scene unfolds to a broad strain in F sharp minor, with the epilogue tending to E minor. Finally, in Act III the orchestral prelude is in a Lydian E major while Cavaradossi's aria is cast in the, for Puccini, rare key of B minor;[6] the actual love scene begins in F major ('O dolci mani'), moves via E and D flat major to G flat major in its central section ('Amaro sol per te') and ends in the E major of 'Trionfal di nuova speme'; the 'Execution' is in a notional G major. In this examination of key-sequences within each act, I have taken account only of the pieces in closed, self-contained form, since they all centre in a definite tonality. The modulating action-music, on the other hand, in which a number of different motifs follow one another in quick, kaleidoscopic succession and which represents the relatively more 'symphonic' part of the opera, is held together by *tremolo*, the maid-of-all-work in Italian realist opera. In parenthesis, it is interesting to compare the duration of the acts of *Tosca* – Act I lasts c.44 minutes, Act II c.40 minutes and Act III c.28 minutes, so the gradual acceleration of the action and its rapid dénouement can be readily read off.

9 *Musical and dramatic structure*

For this analytical chapter I have chosen from all three acts scenes that seem important from either the musical or the dramatic point of view, or both. Before this, something must be said about the overall musico-dramatic structure of the work. We have noted the striking acceleration of the action in Act III, as compared with the leisurely exposition of the drama in Act I, yet any imbalance that might be felt is deceptive. For Act III makes up for its comparative shortness by the weight of its dramatic happenings – the shooting of Cavaradossi, the discovery of Scarpia's murder and Tosca's suicide. Moreover, there is a certain symmetry and correspondence between the musical structures of the two acts which, though not of the strict Bergian order, is marked enough to reinforce my view that *Tosca* is one of the best constructed operas in the repertory. Consider: both acts open, after preliminaries, with an aria for the tenor which is followed by a love duet for soprano and tenor, and both close with a *coup de théâtre* – the *Te Deum* scene of Act I and the execution and suicide of Act III. In the context of the drama the closely corresponding scenes stand worlds apart. Yet Cavaradossi's 'Recondita armonia' and 'E lucevan le stelle' express in their different way the same thing – his all-consuming love for Tosca. Again, the common denominator of the two love scenes is the lovers' romantic illusion in the midst of reality, a reality of which they are not yet aware in Act I – hence the sensuousness, radiance and warmth of the first love duet. In Act III their illusion is the more pathetic because of the deception that the dead Scarpia will play on them; hence, the second love duet is deliberately fragmentary (see Puccini's letter to Ricordi, p. 21) and lacks the sinewy strength of the first love scene, for which it makes up, however, by its tenderness and intimacy. A last point: in Act I Scarpia exposes his diabolical plan – in Act III this is realized but in a manner not allowed for in his scheme. In a sense Act III may be perceived as the *distorted* mirror image of Act I.

101

I shall take the closely corresponding scenes together, and then discuss Scarpia's monologue of Act I, the torture scene and the *scène à faire* of Act II, and finally the Prelude to Act III, the execution and the close of the opera.

(a) Cavaradossi's 'Recondita armonia' and 'E lucevan le stelle'

Both arias arise directly from the situation, and both express Cavaradossi's love for Tosca. The first is, moreover, firmly anchored in the action through the Sacristan's accusatory interjections. Cavaradossi sings it by way of comment on what the cleric has said to him about the 'unknown lady' whose features he recognizes in the painting of Mary Magdalene. Despite its opening words, the aria shows no 'recondite' harmony, being in a plain F major, which key it scarcely leaves. The music displays the same charm and the same degree of *morbidezza* as Rodolfo's 'Nei cieli bigi' in Act I of *Bohème*, with which it also shares a swaying 6/8 movement and a flat key. The text consists of two five-line stanzas which yield a simple binary form, the last sixteen bars of which are given over to the Sacristan. Each of the two sections is preceded by an orchestral ritornello which seems to represent the painter's brush-strokes as they gently pass over the canvas. Noteworthy here are the organum-like progressions in parallel fourths and fifths which lend the music a somewhat archaic air.[1] At the words 'e te, beltade ignota' ('and you, unknown beauty') Puccini weaves imperceptibly into the music the motif of the Attavanti (Ex. 6), and it is good musical psychology that at the

Ex. 6 'Attavanti' theme

e   te, bel-ta - de i - gno - ta,____ cin-ta di chio-me bion - de

mention of Tosca's name Cavaradossi's part should leap a sixth upwards to the only top B flat of the piece, a piece that has the winning simplicity of an Italian folksong.

It is worth remaining for a moment with Example 6. It does not stand out from the rest of the music, and is therefore likely to be heard by most listeners as forming part of the *Gestalt* of the aria which centres on the mysterious ability of art to combine two such contrasting beauties (Attavanti and Tosca) in one portrait. That Puccini does not give the Attavanti a conspicuous theme of her own seems to serve as an indication of the fact that she does not appear in the opera but is a mere reference in the text. She leads a shadowy existence and this Puccini projects most aptly, as seen in the above example, which occurs thrice more in the dialogue between Scarpia and Tosca of Act II where there is talk of the Attavanti, and in the fact that two of Angelotti's themes do service for her, too (Act I).

With Cavaradossi's farewell aria we enter the totally contrasted world of despair. In marked contrast to 'Recondita armonia', Puccini carefully prepares 'E lucevan le stelle' by anticipating its theme in a *sviolinata* in E minor, and as Cavaradossi asks the gaoler's permission to write a note to a 'person dear to me' the 'Love' theme (Ex. 4e) steals in on four solo cellos (*dolcissimo espressivo*) with painful suspensions in the harmony. The text of the aria recalls Dante's famous line that there is no greater sorrow than to recall a time of happiness in misery. 'E lucevan le stelle' creates the impression of an improvisation, as though the words came to Cavaradossi on the spur of the moment. This improvisatory element dictates the structure of the music. While his first-act aria is built up of regular four-bar phrases suggesting that Puccini, consciously or otherwise, equated happiness with a balanced structure, the third-act aria unfolds in the 'irrational' phrasing of $5+7+3$ bars and its repeat: $5+7+6$. This, combined with the gypsy-like *rubato*, seems a striking reflexion of the disturbed state of Cavaradossi's mind at this point of the drama.

The aria opens in a beautiful and unusual way: the warm, sensuous solo clarinet conjures up Cavaradossi's farewell to Tosca with the melody to which the voice subsequently sings a recitative in reiterated notes, each phrase entering after the downbeat throughout its first half. Momentarily D minor is brought in within the orbit of B minor, adding a fresh harmonic colour; noteworthy, too, is the contrast between the vocal part in the two stanzas. In the first, Cavaradossi recites his words pensively against the orchestral melody, in the second stanza he takes it over, *con grande sentimento*, the strings doubling it in two octaves so as to add greater intensity to the vocal phrases. The accompaniment is weighted down almost throughout by trailing syncopations. This *Andante lento* is an outstanding example of the Puccinian lament, reserved for a character in an extreme situation – death or suicide. Its hallmarks are a minor key (here B minor), a slow, dragging pace and the tendency of the melody to sag after having been forcibly pushed upwards. Utter sadness and despair emanate from the music – in the case of Cavaradossi's lament it is naked despair crying out loud, which tempts many tenors to a hysterical rendering. A French commentator[2] with an anti-Puccinian bias once described a particular inflexion in this aria as a 'hoquet tragique' – 'tragic hiccup' – to be found also in other Italian realist operas such as Leoncavallo's *Pagliacci*:

Ex. 17 (a)*Tosca* (b) *Pagliacci*

O   lan-gui-de ca - rez-ze   Ve - sti la giub-ba

Both Puccini's and Leoncavallo's arias are melodic verismo at its most telling.

(b) The two love scenes (Acts I and III)

I avoid speaking in *Tosca* of love duets, as they are usually called, since Tosca and Cavaradossi rarely sing together, the essence of a true duet, but alternate with each other in a kind of duologue. Realist opera, probably following Wagner, eschews concerted numbers for the soloists, as this does not conform to the axiom of dramatic truth.

The two love scenes represent the lyrical core of the acts. In both, the lovers are shown to be in the grip of emotion for each other, yet the situations in which they find themselves in Acts I and III are vastly different. In the first love scene the sun still seems to shine bright and clear – they feel secure in their love and their life. In the second scene dark clouds have gathered and, despite the safe-conduct in Tosca's hand, they feel, after their grim experiences in Act II, a great disquiet if not indeed an unconscious threat – Tosca because she is haunted by the fear that something may go wrong with the mock-execution, and Cavaradossi perhaps because in his heart of hearts he has a suspicion that he will be shot in earnest. This difference in the psychology behind the two situations has determined the difference in lyrical style and expression.

We note, first, the disproportion in length of the two scenes. That in Act I is 258 bars long, as against the 145 bars of that in Act III. The first scene is one of the longest in middle-period Puccini and this was probably dictated by the composer's desire to show the lovers' mutual intensity of feeling, in order to make Tosca's murder of Scarpia plausible. Puccini's thought may have been that only a woman so deeply in love would have the moral strength, first to agree to Scarpia's bargain and then to kill him. There are four lyrical sections in the first love scene which are twice interrupted by recitative-cum-ariosi:

1. Tosca's 'entrance' music – A flat major (23 bars)
   Recitative/arioso (27 bars)
2. Tosca's arietta 'Non la sospiri' – D flat major (51 bars)
   Recitative/arioso (80 bars)
3. Cavaradossi's arietta 'Qual occhio al mondo' – E flat major (23 bars)
4. Duet, 'Mia gelosa!' – E major – (F major) – E major (54 bars)

Our main concern will be the way in which Puccini holds the four sections together and moulds them into a musico-dramatic unity. His first means is thematic relationship between the themes of Tosca and Cavaradossi (Exx. 4b–d). His second and more important one is to establish coherence by key-relationship. The first three sections, all in flat keys, are ranged together according to the scheme: tonic, subdominant and dominant, which is clear evidence that in *Tosca* Puccini still relies on traditional classical procedures. I am naturally referring here only to the 'closed' lyrical forms with their definite tonalities, and disregarding the intervening recitatives-cum-ariosi with their free-ranging modulations. The seemingly puzzling point in the love scene is the key of section 4 – E major. This could of course be explained by *Terzrückung* or shift of a third from A flat (section 1) or a chromatic screwing up of E flat (section 3). But whatever the theoretical explication, a glance at the text gives a dramatic reason for Puccini's key-scheme. Tosca's 'Entrance' music (Ex. 4b) is based on an orchestral theme – an indication that his invention was frequently primarily instrumental.[3] In it she first gives vent to her jealous suspicion and then, after telling Cavaradossi the reason for her unexpected visit, embarks on a solo piece in D flat major in which she evokes the romantic charm of their villa in the country (Ex. 4c). Her jealousy is re-aroused by seeing the painting of the Mary Magdalene–Attavanti, but Cavaradossi calms her with his arietta, 'Qual occhio al mondo', in E flat major (Ex. 4d). Until now we have had essentially solo pieces, and exchanges between the two in recitatives/ariosi. To raise the emotional temperature, Puccini crowns the scene with a climax – 'Mia gelosa!' in E major, which is more of a real duet, with his and her phrases following each other very closely and joining in a unison. The climactic effect lies not only in the expansive and lovely new melody (Ex. 4e) but also in the choice of a completely new key for this last section. For Puccini, E major seems to have been a luminous key[4] associated with the expression of ardour and joyful exaltation, and it is no coincidence that the end of the love scene in Act III, the unison 'Trionfal di nuova speme' (Ex. 4k), is in the same key.

Let me return for a moment to the E major section of the first-act duet. Cavaradossi repeats the 'Mia gelosa' melody as a kind of solo in F major, a key chosen by Puccini to introduce tonal contrast as well as to allow the tenor a high B flat (just as he does in 'Recondita armonia' which is in F major), this high note being secure with most tenors; the love scene ends in E major, to be regarded as the home-key of this last section. I hesitate, however, to relate the E major tonality in the two love scenes to the ending of the 'Scarpia' motto on the E major chord as does Roger Parker who interprets this as suggesting the 'fatal triangle' (Scarpia–Tosca–Cavaradossi) (p. 126). This is of course a perfectly acceptable suggestion from the semantic point of view. Yet, in view of the multi-determined nature of key symbolisms, I am inclined to see in the E major chord of the 'Scarpia' motto, notably as it is stated in its sustained form at the opening of the opera, the projection of the might and immense self-confidence of the Roman Chief of Police. In other words, the same key seems to me also to have different meanings depending on the context in which it occurs.

To sum up. This love scene is masterfully conceived and executed, with the lyrical element predominating, but it is never allowed to spread itself unduly and is always interrupted at the right moment by recitatives/ariosi in which the action moves forward. The whole scene is comparable to a poem in rhyming stanzas interspersed with prose passages. As for its lyrical ideas, they are marked by a singular radiance, sensuous warmth and strength of line projecting the lovers' as yet unclouded happiness. All of this contrasts strongly with the love scene of Act III which consists of three main lyrical sections:

1. Cavaradossi's 'O dolci mani' – F major (20 bars)
   Arioso (33 bars)
2. Cavaradossi's 'Amaro sol per' – G flat major (34 bars)
   Recitative/arioso (24 bars)
3. Unison, 'Trionfal di nuova speme' – E major (20 bars)
4. Recitative (14 bars)

Like the love scene of Act I, here too the flat keys are followed by a final section in E major, but in the changed situation the lyrical effusions are shorter and, instead of sensuousness and vigour, tenderness and *morbidezza* prevail, to say nothing of the intentional fragmentation caused by Tosca's constant preoccupation with her lover's mock execution.

'O dolci mani' is gentle, caressing music, characteristically broken off on the dominant of its home-key by Tosca's impatient 'Senti, l'ora è vicina' and her instruction to Cavaradossi on how to simulate his death after the shooting, at which point Puccini quotes the 'Deception' figure (Ex. 14) by way of an ironic comment. The theme of Tosca's arioso (Ex. 16) obstinately returns to the note D flat, suggesting her nagging thought that Cavaradossi should fall naturally. The central section of this scene is preceded by a kind of intermezzo in E major/D flat major, 'Liberi! Via pel mar!' ('Free! Away to the sea!'). in which the composer could not resist the temptation to add an unnecessary illustrative touch by evoking in the orchestra the rocking movements of the ship on the waves. 'Amaro sol per te' represents the lyrical core of the scene which he took over (in harmony and orchestration) from the original Act IV of *Edgar*. The first half is sung by Cavaradossi and the second by Tosca, and there is great delicacy and suppleness in the vocal phrasing; in its mixture of diatonic scale-segments and wide intervals and the presence of a *gruppetto*-like figure (*x*) it conforms to the specific melodic style of *Tosca*:

Ex. 18

Recalled to reality, Tosca repeats, with great unease, her instruction to her lover to fall naturally and at the right moment, with the 'Instruction' theme (Ex. 16) now moved up a semitone as if to suggest her increased concern. In this arioso Cavaradossi's answer is marked *'triste'*, indicating his foreboding of death.

Section 3, 'Trionfal di nuova speme', is a rousing but somewhat rhetorical hymn sung in unison by the lovers (Ex. 4k), but, revealingly, Puccini did not provide an orchestral accompaniment for its major part, possibly wanting to imply that their thoughts of freedom and love are without any foundation in reality.

In the closing recitative (section 4) Tosca admonishes her lover for the last time to fall correctly after the firing to which Cavaradossi laughingly replies 'Come la Tosca in teatro', and not to move until she has given him a sign (Ex. 16 in C major). Follows the ominous *Largo con gravità*.

(c) Finale of Act I

In the score, this scene, comprising Scarpia's first monologue sung against the background of church music and culminating in the imposing *Te Deum*, is marked 'Finale I', which suggests that Puccini's original intention may have been to name the close of the following two acts as 'Finale II' and 'Finale III' respectively – an indication that, despite the daring novelty of the subject, he was then still thinking in terms of the traditional Italian opera. This *Adagio religioso* extends to 85 bars, of which over 70 rest on the bass pedal B flat – F, sounded by a low bell. Could it be that he wanted to suggest the unshakeable pillars on which the might of the Roman Catholic Church stands? The contrapuntal writing (such as there is) shows that his training at Lucca in the craft of his four ancestors, all church composers, was thorough. The two themes which form antecedent and consequent (Ex. 4f) dominate the music until Scarpia joins the chorus in the second verse of the *Te Deum*. All stops are pulled out (full orchestra, organ, bells, cannon-shots and a stage band of four horns and three trombones for the *Te Deum*) to conjure up the pomp and circumstance of the occasion. Yet what of Scarpia? Has he been adequately portrayed in the music? According to the stage-direction he is in turn to be 'smiling sardonically' and 'ironic' ('Va, Tosca!'), 'ferocious' ('A doppia mira'), 'seized by erotic passion' ('illanguidir con spasimo d'amore') and 'as if awakening from a dream' ('Tosca, mi fai dimenticare Iddio!'). Rarely has an operatic scene offered such an opportunity for the musical suggestion of *both* the sacred and the profane. But Puccini has not seized it, for Scarpia's swift-changing moods are only in the stage-directions, not in the music. Admittedly, there are a few leaps up to E flat and F to suggest his excitement, but almost throughout, the voce-part follows the religious vein of the orchestral music. In other words, the composer avoids one of the most difficult problems of dramatic composition–the *simultaneous* projection of two opposingworlds. It would have needed a Wagner or a Verdi to do full justice to this scene. Puccini, the born man of the theatre, achieves his effects by a well-calculated combination of *extra*-musical means – scenic, histrionic and verbal. Scenic, by setting a scheming satyr against a religious background; histrionic, by relying on a singer–actor's gestures and facial expressions; verbal, by allowing Scarpia's words to be heard distinctly over the toneless murmur of the chorus and the greatly reduced dynamics of the orchestra. It is not until Scarpia joins the chorus in the *Te Deum*, that is, at the point where his erotic fantasies are replaced by a religious sentiment, that character and music coincide. Puccini's main concern in this finale was evidently to close the act with an impressive *scenic* spectacle in which his sense of the *optique du théâtre* triumphed, and so he created one of the most effective act-endings in all opera. It is Puccini at his Meyerbeerian best, which is unquestionably better than the best of Meyerbeer.

(d) The Torture scene and *scène à faire* (Act II)

Of the four scenes which comprise Act II, the last two are the most important from a musico-dramatic point of view and contain the most dynamic passages of the opera.

Tosca has arrived in Scarpia's room and, before being led away to the torture chamber, Cavaradossi whispers to her to say not a word about Angelotti. The sombre, brooding and claustrophobic atmosphere, in which the dialogue between Scarpia and Tosca is to unfold, is set in an orchestral introduction in G minor scored in intimate chamber-music style. The sense of pain emanating from it crystallizes in a sighing appoggiatura. This 'Pain' motif shows how Puccini, by inserting a tiny detail in the melody, namely an augmented instead of a major second (C sharp-B flat), whose first note forms a tritone with the bass G, greatly intensifies its expressive force. When the 'Pain' motif is first heard in E minor in the previous scene, it is marked *molto espressivo, lamentoso* (Ex. 10), and it recurs three times while Cavaradossi is under torture.

The dialogue between Scarpia and Tosca opens with an insinuating barcarolle-like idea (B flat major) in a smoothly flowing 6/8 time in which Scarpia, with well-simulated amiability and politeness (*con gentilezza e galanteria*) attempts to put Tosca at her ease. But he soon shows his real nature in the 'Torture' music whose D minor theme (Ex. 4i) on violins and cellos is made more ferocious (scale-segment again) by the 'cutting' figures on the violas. There are two repeats of that theme. The first occurs when Scarpia speaks of the steel circlet round Cavaradossi's brow which at every new denial cuts deeper into his flesh, illustrated by the demisemiquaver runs linking the main notes of the theme. At Tosca's cry 'Non è ver, non è ver' there is a cruel wrench from D minor to C minor which takes on the character almost of a *leit*-harmony since it recurs again in Act III, in Tosca's account to her lover of how she killed Scarpia. The second repeat is at rehearsal no. 35 when Scarpia rises to a pitch of fury at

Tosca's refusal to betray Angelotti's hiding-place. The D minor theme is now extended to cover scalewise the range of two full octaves and the linking runs are greatly lengthened, with the orchestra in full uproar until the climax is reached in Tosca's violent outcries – a typical illustration of melodic verismo (Ex. 11). At the end of this passage, according to Father Panichelli, who was present at a piano rehearsal with the singers, Puccini hit the keyboard with his first and in an access of megalomaniac pride exclaimed: 'Questa musica la può scrivere Dio, e poi io!' – 'God can write this music and after him only me!'.[5] The point about this scene is that, despite its emotional excess, Puccini writes music which remains fully valid as music and can readily be analysed as such – it never descends to noise. As Mozart said in a letter to his father of 26 September 1791: 'Passion whether violent or not must never be expressed in such a way as to excite disgust and as music, even in the most terrible situations, must never offend the ear, but must please the hearer or, in other words, must never cease to be *music*'. That is the case with the 'Torture' music in *Tosca*.

Tosca can bear no more, and reveals Angelotti's hideout. Puccini's timing here is perfect. There are nearly 20 bars for the tremendous agitation of the previous scene to subside, the music coming to a halt on Spoletta's Latin prayer, *ppp*. A general pause, and on a tutti *ff* the 'Well' motif (Ex. 1b) crashes in, followed by Tosca saying rapidly in a suffocated voice on a repeated low E, 'Nel pozzo . . . nel giardino'– 'In the well . . . in the garden'. Later Scarpia repeats her words in a loud voice (on high notes) followed by the extended 'Well' motif. The effect is shattering. Sciarrone's news of the victory of Napoleon is the cue for Cavaradossi's stentorian outburst, 'Vittoria! Vittoria!', Puccini introducing his theme (Ex. 4a) in full panoply, with the four trombones thundering out the melody while the rest of the wind hammer away at an incisive rhythm; the passage gives the impression of being armour-clad. The subsequent trio, 'L'alba vindice appar', is the only concerted piece for the three soloists in the whole opera. It is a march-like, driving piece in B flat minor, symbolizing Cavaradossi's defiance of Scarpia and his paean to liberty, culminating in Tosca's 'Agony' theme (Ex. 11), whose motivation lies in Scarpia's command to send her lover to the gallows. The psychological implausibility of Cavaradossi's tremendous access of enthusiasm has already been remarked upon.

We now arrive at the *scène à faire* which begins at no. 45 with the smoothly flowing barcarolle which opened Scarpia's first conversation with Tosca (p. 109), now transposed from B flat major to A major, the bight key, possibly suggesting that Scarpia feels nearer to his aim. The central piece of this scene is his monologue 'Già. Mi dicon venal', which is in ternary form (A–B–A). A is a free arioso introducing Scarpia's 'Lust' motif (Ex. 12). There is a striking affinity with the opening of the 'Cavaradossi' theme (Ex. 4a) – both start with stepwise descending minims – and I suggest that Puccini, by this affinity, wanted to hint, consciously or otherwise, at Scarpia's expectation for a brief moment that he might take the place of Tosca's lover. Subsequently, the descending seconds of Ex. 12a are widened

Ex. 12 'Lust' motif

Ex. 4a 'Cavaradossi' theme

to descending fourths (Ex. 12b) as if to indicate Scarpia's waxing lust. It seems strange, however, that Puccini should here resort to the contrapuntal device of inverting (upside down) Ex. 12 (at 'moneta, no! no!') and that the motif should recall a fugal subject.

B is the lyrical middle section of the monologue ('Già mi struggea'), an *Andante appassionato* in G flat major (Ex. 4h). Like Scarpia's first monologue in this act, this is not of Puccini's best vintage, but it projects well his growing sexual excitement, as witness the high tessitura of the vocal line, the restless string syncopations and the wrench from G flat major to A major to A flat major. The *Andante* is open-ended and flows without a break or caesura into the return of section A, as if to suggest Scarpia's continuous and rising desire. A is much shortened, with the descending fourths now blazed out by the whole orchestra and the voice part reaching up to G flat, the only place in the entire opera in which Scarpia has that high note. Scarpia, now at the height of his sexual paroxysm, makes his second advance on Tosca, when suddenly the sound of distant drums is heard (not in Sardou). At one stroke the situation changes dramatically; first, the sound stops his pursuit of Tosca and, second, it provides him with a further turn of the screw, for the drums, he explains, mean that her lover is being led to the gallows. His explanation pro-

ceeds to one of those sinister themes for which *Tosca* is conspicuous
– a five-bar strain in the Phrygian mode alternating with a woodwind
appoggiatura against which the off-stage drums continue:

Ex. 13 'Gallows' motif

Tosca's aria follows. 'Vissi d'arte' is often, erroneously, called a
'preghiera' or 'prayer', but the text makes it abundantly clear that it is
a plaint or lament addressed to God for having repaid her so cruelly
for her good deeds. It is strange, however, that the composer has
musically so little fresh to say in a situation that might have been
expected to fire his imagination. The only new idea is the eight-bar
introduction in E flat minor whose progression of faburden-like
chords gives it a somewhat ecclesiastical flavour. The main section,
in the major, is built up of regular four-bar phrases derived from
Tosca's 'Entrance' music (Ex. 4b) on to which at the end is tagged her
'Agony' motif (Ex. 11). To be sure, the literal repetition of previously
heard material is defensible on the ground of dramatic relevance, but
in this particular case it smacks of labour-saving. Vocally, 'Vissi
d'arte' is a splendid piece, demanding of the singer a perfect *legato*
and radiant, liquescent tone. Puccini first merely hints (at 'diedi
fiori') at the later climax which enters at 'perchè, Signor, ah' on a leap
of a sixth upwards to top B flat and then sinks down via A flat to G.
Appropriate to the melody are the soft pastel colours of the composer's orchestral palette.

Tosca's real prayer, addressed to Scarpia, comes in the following
arioso with its sadly drooping fifths ('come un lamento') in which a
tonal variant of the 'Gallows' motif (Ex. 13) reveals what is going on
in her mind. When subsequently Spoletta enters with the news of
Angelotti's suicide, there is an ironic comment in the orchestra,
which quotes his 'Escape' theme (Ex. 2c) as if Puccini meant to say,
yes, Angelotti managed to escape Scarpia's clutches but only in this
way. Tosca gives her silent consent to the shameful bargain in a *Lento
doloroso* of two bars which represent a free inversion of the 'Pain'
motif (Ex. 10) played now by four solo strings. When Tosca requests
that *afterwards* Cavaradossi should be freed at once and Scarpia

replies that this cannot be done and that his death must be simulated, there appears in the orchestra a most insignificant-seeming figure of a rising minor third – the 'Deception' motif (Ex. 14) which will recur in full force at the execution in Act III. Here it creates a bitonal clash with the *tremolo* chord (A minor against D minor). This is an example of Puccini's use of the simplest of means to give Scarpia's command to Spoletta to shoot Cavaradossi 'like Count Palmieri' an ominous undercurrent which is heightened by the scoring of the motif for cellos and basses, *p, pizz.*

Scarpia's writing of the safe-conduct proceeds to a beautifully shaped melody in F sharp minor spun out to 14 bars. It is played by the muted first violins on the G string and doubled by the violas; this imparts to the theme a markedly dark sonority which, together with its melancholy expression, makes it one of the outstanding inventions in the opera:

Ex. 15 'Murder' theme

Yet, in my opinion, it does not quite fit the melodic style of *Tosca*, and on internal evidence it would appear to date back to the time of *Manon Lescaut*; it may have been written for the final act of that opera in which the key of F sharp minor, a relatively rare key in Puccini, is important.

Scarpia's murder is accompanied by sheer situation music in pure verismo style – realistic shouts and groans in the voice-part and a noisy chaotic rhythm in the orchestra, until a descending whole-tone scale marks his demise. Example 15 recurs a little later in a *sviolinata* doubled by cor anglais and clarinets, yet this orchestral intensification seems entirely unmotivated since for 7 out of 12 bars it accompanies trivial stage-business (i.e. Tosca cleaning her hands of Scarpia's blood and putting her hair in order before a mirror). In the Epilogue, however, music and action are again in total harmony with each other. After Tosca has uttered her toneless phrase, 'E avanti a lui tremava tutta Roma!', which tempts some singers to shout it out in rhetorical fashion, the orchestra, by quoting Scarpia's 'Lust' (Ex. 12) and Cavaradossi's 'Love' (Ex. 4d) motifs, reveals the direction of her thoughts. When she begins her religious ceremony, the Scarpia motto (Ex. 1a) rises, ghostlike, on the low strings[6] with its third chord, on the woodwind, now in E minor, minor versions having already occurred twice before in the *scène à faire*. (Puccini associates the major with 'being' and the minor with 'non-being', an idea that springs of course from the classical view of the mysterious contrast between the major and minor third.) All is played as softly as possible, then on a sudden *f* chord distant drum rolls are heard (indicated in Sardou) – an ominous portent of Act III. The scene closes in E minor. But, after a general pause bar, there is an abrupt shift to F sharp minor. Puccini may have intended this as a reminder of the key used in Scarpia's murder, or, more probable, as an indication of Tosca softly closing the door behind her and a swift drop of the curtain.

This whole scene is typical Sardou – sheer theatre, made impressive by Puccini's music, which is also noteworthy for its extreme economy of means.

(e) Prelude to Act III

After the events of Act II, Puccini provides relief in the form of a poetic mood-picture evoking the freshness of a Roman dawn to which sheep-bells and the shepherd's sad little song in the Lydian mode on E add a pastoral touch. The composer had asked Zanazzo for some verses in the style of the shepherd songs of the Romagna, verses that made no reference to the drama, and this reinforces the objective character of the Prelude. It is as if Puccini for a moment stepped outside the action, and sought contrast in an independent nature scene. The only reminder of the drama is the Scarpia motto which like a shadow softly steals in for a few bars on a string pizzicato. With a suggestion of scintillating stars (again a stepwise scale descent (Ex. 4j)) and the 'concert' of church bells, Puccini transmogrifies Sardou's prosaic stage-direction into a veritable poem.

(f) Cavaradossi's execution

Tosca contains two of those sinister marches in the invention of which Puccini was an unsurpassed master. The first occurs in the interrogation scene of Act II (Ex. 9a), and the second accompanies the execution and its preparation (Ex. 9b).

This *Largo con gravità* unfolds over a regular 2/4 tread in the bass and with an *ostinato* figure in the melody; these two elements give the music a feeling of inexorability. The march is notated in G major, but is harmonized so as to give the impression of a minor tonality,

Ex. 9a 'Interrogation' motif (march)

Ex. 9b 'Execution' motif

dying away on the A minor chord – the second degree of the notional major key. The texture is occasionally in two real parts, the lower of which produces in the subsequent *ff* version, where it is scored for the two trumpets in octaves, a piercing dissonance. Before the soldiers' fusillade Puccini reintroduces Example 14 (four trombones plus strings, *ff*), as if to say that Scarpia has triumphantly achieved his posthumous deception. Dramatic irony has rarely been used to more impressive effect than at the point when, after the shooting, Tosca says to Cavaradossi, lying on the ground but, she thinks, alive: 'Là, muori! Ecco un artista!' – 'Now, die now! What an artist!' The orchestra answers her by thundering out the march on the four horns in unison, staccato. The impact is almost cataclysmic.

(g) Close of the opera

The ending of *Tosca*, with its reminiscence of Cavaradossi's 'E lucevan le stelle', has troubled me for years. Puccini evidently chose this tune because it is the best and most moving in Act III, possibly in the whole opera. He did do the same with Mimì's 'Sono andati?' in *Bohème* and with the Minstrel's song in *La fanciulla del west*. It seems to have become the practice in veristic opera – as witness the end of *Pagliacci*, with its reminiscence of Canio's 'Vesti la giubba'. Puccini's is certainly an effective close. But is the theme dramatically relevant? Not in my view. For one thing, the tune represents Cavaradossi's farewell to love and life and has nothing to do with Tosca's suicide and, for another, it was never heard by the heroine. A distorted version of the 'Love' theme (Ex. 4e), with searing dissonances in the harmony, would have been more appropriate. But far better motivated would have been a recall of the 'Scarpia' motto

(Ex. 1a) as a last ironic salute from beyond the grave, just as Bizet brings back the 'Carmen' motif at the end of his masterpiece. In this way all three acts of *Tosca* would have terminated in the same manner, and that would have formed a nice symmetry, aesthetically most satisfying. It would also have reminded us that the *fons et origo* of the whole drama is Scarpia. But this is a minor consideration. More important for my argument is a phrase in Sardou. We recall that in the final scene of the play Tosca exclaims to Spoletta and the others, 'Go and see what I have done to the monster who is still able to commit murder though he is dead', a phrase which contains the whole meaning of the last act. Had this phrase (perhaps in a shortened form) been retained in the libretto, might this not have induced Puccini to conclude the opera with the 'Scarpia' motto, which would have provided a far more relevant ending? This would have shown the composer as a true musical dramatist, not merely the man of the theatre relying on sheer effect.

10 *Analysis: Act I in perspective**

BY ROGER PARKER

It is perhaps because of our over-familiarity with Puccini's musical language – and of course its exploitation in the hands of numerous imitators, both in Hollywood and elsewhere – that critical writings on the composer have tended to polarize. On the one hand, there are those who seem to resent profoundly his popular success, who find his music coarse, vulgar and cynical, and who present his image as a blunt stone on which to sharpen their wit. This started almost from the beginning. *La Bohème* and *Tosca*, for example, were initially greeted coolly by the press: both represented a change of direction which the critics found hard to follow.[1] And the eventual canonization of these operas, far from redeeming Puccini in the eyes of the journalists, simply added more fuel to their fire: as his later operas appeared, they were constantly arraigned for falling below the standard of the early works, now proclaimed 'masterpieces'. A little later, the Italian critic Fausto Torrefranca devoted a full-length book to the composer. It turns out to be a polemic of rare severity: a study whose approach to its subject is almost entirely negative. As Torrefranca says in his Preface, he chose Puccini because: 'he seems to me the composer who personifies with greatest completeness the decadence of today's Italian music, and who represents its cynical commercialism, its lamentable impotence, its celebration of the international vogue'.[2] Torrefranca's book is an interesting document of Italian cultural history, marking as it does a step from the cosy – if bombastic – chauvinism of the 1880s and 1890s towards the more sinister xenophobia of the 1920s: but its choice of Puccini as the whipping-boy seems symptomatic. Moving to more recent times, we find that the critical barrage has continued unabated. For Stravinsky, *La fanciulla del west* was 'a remarkably up-to-date TV horse opera' and (because of its similarity to *Madama Butterfly*) 'really an Eastern western'.[3] For Joseph Kerman, *Tosca* is 'that shabby little shocker', and in the final scene of the opera, when the heroine

117

launches herself from the parapets of the Castel Sant'Angelo to a triumphant reprise of 'E lucevan le stelle', 'the orchestra screams the first thing that comes into its head'.[4]

On the other hand, we have a fair number of supporters, often of necessity self-styled defenders. There have been reasoned general assessments from several authors, including Wilfrid Mellers, William Austin and Donald Grout (although the last of these cannot entirely eschew a tone of moral censure when he identifies 'a kind of perpetual pregnancy in the melody').[5] But the best of the specialists (one thinks in particular of Claudio Sartori and Mosco Carner), though often percipient on matters of general style, rarely find time to approach individual passages in any great detail.[6] One might be excused for assuming that Puccini represents a last outpost against the rigours of music theory – the immediacy of his music unnerving even the most catholic of analysts. In such a context, the present chapter can do no more than explore a few of the analytical possibilities presented by *Tosca*; attempt a discussion of the music in which general issues and value judgements, though necessarily addressed, will be peripheral to precise details of the score. So far as is possible, and of course the term is only relative, an 'objective' assessment is offered. In order to achieve as close a focus as possible, I have limited my remarks to Act I of the opera, and concentrated on three broad areas: the relationship between words and music; the interaction of tonality and drama; and the function of motif.

Words and music

You want a 'lyrical piece' (*pezzo lirico*) and you understand that a 'lyrical piece' is something that has nothing to do with psychology or with the drama. So 'lyrical piece' it will be. And, to please you, I have even followed faithfully the metrical scheme you sent me. Prosody doesn't come out of it too well, but the 'lyrical piece' cares not a jot for prosody.

Giacosa to Giulio Ricordi
(9 September 1898)[7]

Giuseppe Giacosa's complaint is one of many. Throughout Puccini's career, his collaborations with librettists were fraught with problems; and no more so than during this period, in which he was confident enough to know what he wanted, but in which his musical style was relatively unfamiliar. As the letter shows, Giacosa was especially sensitive in matters of literary honour, and letters of proffered resignation litter the Puccini *Carteggio*; but he was not alone in suffering such frustrations. On the evidence of the composer's correspondence, the task of supervising progress from an initial dramatic idea to a finished libretto constituted Puccini's greatest creative struggle.

The reasons for this tension and difficulty are complex, and not easily explained. Most basic was the composer's initial attitude to an operatic subject. Puccini's essential priority when examining possible sources for a new opera was not one of immediate concern to his librettists. They would look above all for a satisfying dramatic structure within which there was room for a suitable variety of effect and situation. He, on the other hand, was primarily concerned with finding an ambience which could stimulate his musical imagination in new directions. If, for example, we examine the operas from *La Bohème* onwards, the most noticeable difference between individual works is not one of character or situation, but of setting: bohemian Paris; Rome in 1800; Japan; the Californian Gold Rush, etc. Each is characterized by its location and, most important, there is an increasing tendency for each location to carry its own musical analogue – an immediately identifiable translation in musical terms. A comparison with Verdi is instructive. While Verdi's plot settings were on occasion changed at the last moment with no lasting damage to the work's integrity, such alterations would be unthinkable for all Puccini's mature operas. It is perhaps significant that the one work of Verdi's which could under no circumstances be transplanted is *Aida*, the opera which first inspired Puccini to become a dramatic composer.

This overriding concern with ambience is, in my opinion, closely connected with Puccini's awareness of his own musical limitations, of the fact that his musical style was not sufficiently flexible to allow complex musical distinctions between the various characters of an opera. If the individuals tend always to be subsumed under an overall atmosphere, then their lack of differentiation becomes less of a problem, the effort of finding something new – some defining new musical gesture – need be made only once for each opera. Resources are husbanded. As the gradual slowing of Puccini's creative output shows, even this single effort became ever more difficult to effect, and his endless picking-over of operatic subjects becomes a reflection of musical sterility as much as of dramatic fastidiousness. Whatever the reasons, the immediate result of such a preoccupation was to make the composer occasionally indifferent to matters which his librettists considered crucial and conditioning. The fact that, in *Tosca*, Scarpia has two arias 'back-to-back' (at the end of Act I and the beginning of Act II) was something which outraged Giacosa's sense of dramatic propriety; but it seemed of little consequence to Puccini. Nor did he mind that Act I, and to a limited extent Acts II and III , are a succession of duologues: the more characters become at one with the ambience, the less important is their particular disposition in one place or another. Understandably, such differences of priority led to disagreements and misunderstandings, particularly for Giacosa, as he seems not to have been granted a hearing of the music until rather late in the day.

This was only the first difficulty which arose between the composer and his librettists. Once Puccini had decided on his subject, music often seemed to arrive without the stimulus of words. Time and again, the poets were expected to fit words to existing music, a process which required submission not only to a strict metrical pattern, but often to a particular sequence of vowels. The most famous instance is in Act II of *La Bohème*, in which the opening words of Musetta's famous waltz, 'Quando m'en vo, quando m'en vo soletta', started life in Puccinian doggerel as 'Coccoricó, coccoricó, bistecca' ('Cock-adoodle-do, cock-adoodle-do, beefsteak'). Furthermore, Puccini was little less than fanatical in his search for the precisely suitable word or phrase. Some thirty years before *Tosca*, Verdi had spoken to his librettist for *Aida*, Ghislanzoni, of the 'parola scenica', the 'theatrical word' or 'scenic utterance': it was a term he coined to describe a 'word that clarifies and presents the situation neatly and plainly',[8] something to be used at a point of culmination, a succinct verbal summary of one particular strand of the drama. In Puccini's case one has the impression that every word was a potential 'parola scenica', that librettists were no longer allowed to lapse into the verbal divagations and octosyllabic knitting of their forebears.

A comparison of the first act libretti of *Tosca* and *Aida* may at this point be instructive, demonstrating something of the added problems with which the Puccinian librettists had to contend.[9] Act I of *Aida* has 181 lines which, according to custom, were divided into two broad types. Seventy-seven lines are *versi sciolti*, freely alternating seven- and eleven-syllable lines, usually unrhymed. They were used in recitative passages, where the music is rhythmically least tied. The remaining 114 lines are *versi lirici*, which are of fixed line length (either five, six, seven, eight, ten or eleven syllables per line), arranged in stanzas, and with a rhyme scheme of some kind.[10] A good example of both types comes in Radames's first solo, in which the *versi sciolti* of his recitative turn to the *versi lirici* of 'Celeste Aida':

Ramfis:	Giovane e prode è desso – Ora del Nume	11
	Reco i decreti al Re.	
Radames:	Se quel guerriero	11
	Io fossi! se il mio sogno	7
	Si avverasse! . . . Un esercito di prodi	11
	Da me guidato . . . e la vittoria – e il plauso	11
	Di Menfi tutta! – E a te, mia dolce Aida,	11
	Tornar di lauri cinto . . .	7
	Dirti: per te ho pugnato e per te ho vinto!	11
	Celeste Aida, forma divina,	10
	Mistico serto di luce e fior;	10
	Del mio pensiero tu sei regina,	10
	Tu di mia vita sei lo splendor.[11]	10

The first act of *Tosca* is markedly different. It has 335 lines, nearly twice as many as *Aida*, though the number in *versi lirici* is much reduced, to only 68 lines. The main body of the text is thus in *versi sciolti*. The reason for the overall increase of text is plain: there is very little word repetition in *Tosca*, and so text is consumed at a greater rate. This immediately makes the librettist's task more arduous: he has simply more words to produce. But the principal problem lies in the changed nature of the *versi sciolti*. In *Aida* they typically act as a prosaic counterpart to *versi lirici* and, as we see from the Radames example quoted above, are usually unrhymed until the final couplet. In *Tosca*, presumably in part to compensate for the relative scarcity of *versi lirici*, rhyme becomes an important element of the *versi sciolti*, making them more 'poetic'. This change is naturally a direct reflection of the change in musical style from middle-period Verdi to Puccini: just as the distinction between recitative and aria was becoming increasingly blurred, so there was a gradual merging of the verse forms which by tradition had underpinned them. Often in *Tosca* one finds a kind of mutant form: elements of regular rhythmic stress, and frequent use of end rhymes (hallmarks of *versi lirici*), act within the alternating seven- and eleven-syllable format of *versi sciolti*. Take, for example, the beginning of the Act I love duet, in which all but the first line are rhymed, but in which no fixed pattern of line length or rhythmic stress emerges:

Tosca:	Mario!	
Cavaradossi:	Son qui!	
Tosca:	Perchè chiuso?	
Cavaradossi:	Lo vuole	11
	il Sagrestano.	

Tosca:	A chi parlavi?	
Cavaradossi:	A te!	11
Tosca:	Altre parole bisbigliavi. Ov'è? . . .	11
Cavaradossi:	Chi?	
Tosca:	Colei! . . . Quella donna! . . .	7
	Ho udito i lesti	5
	passi e un fruscio di vesti . . .	7
Cavaradossi:	Sogni!	
Tosca:	Lo neghi?	5
Cavaradossi:	Lo nego e t'amo!	
Tosca:	Oh! innanzi la madonna.	11
	Lascia pria ch'io l'infiori e che la preghi.[12]	11

Clearly passages such as this reflect a compromise: although the words fall into no traditional prosodic pattern, literary honour is in part placated by the injection of some level of purely verbal organization. The anomalous five-syllable line 'Ho udito i lesti' is balanced by a line of similar length, 'Sogni! / Lo neghi?'; the rhymes (some of which, given their syntactic position, could not conceivably be illustrated in the music) are gestures towards the poetic – rather than an element of the poetry – but nevertheless serve as an indication of literary attitude. Above all they tell us that men such as Giacosa considered themselves part of a poetic tradition when writing libretti; and given so draconian a collaborator as Puccini, their attempts command a certain admiration. The effect is similar to that of a poetic translation which attempts to retain the line length and rhyme scheme of the original poem: judged as pure poetry, the result will be largely uninspired, at times risible; but the fact that it has been done at all cannot, in the circumstances, fail to impress.

One curious feature, in part brought about by the presence of rhymes in what is otherwise free verse, is that even though the overall effect of a Puccini libretto may be of a prosaic genre, lacking in rhythmic definition, certain passages are more formal than one might traditionally expect. In the opening scene of Act I, for example, Angelotti's breathless remarks sound curiously 'pat' because of their rhyming couplets (in this quotation I have omitted the copious stage directions):

Ah! . . . Finalmente! . . . Nel terror mio stolto	11
vedea ceffi di birro in ogni volto.	11
La pila . . . la colonna . . .	7
'A piè della Madonna'	7
mi scrisse mia sorella . . .	7
Ecco la chiave . . . ed ecco la cappella! . . . [13]	11

It should come as no surprise that, especially in serious moments,

Puccini does not often draw attention to these rhyming couplets in his musical setting: rhymes have a way of sounding comic when used obtrusively in a musical context. Their occasional use is for a particular dramatic effect (the opening couplet of the above quotation); or to underline an ironic moment, such as the Sacristan's:

> Di quell'ignota
> che i dì passati a pregar qui venìa
> tutta devota – e pia.[14]

where the ornamental, 'Baroque' cadence makes a rhyme appropriate (15/3/1–2).[15] Sometimes Puccini will exploit a rhyme when it concludes a discrete section of dialogue, as an added mark of punctuation (17/2/3–18/1/1)

> *Sagrestano*:   (Fuori, Satana, fuori!)
> *Cavaradossi*:   Dammi i colori![16]

But if the 'action' scenes are rather more formal than might be expected, at least by the standards of earlier nineteenth-century Italian opera, in the arias the reverse is the case. The first section of sustained lyricism, Cavaradossi's 'Recondita armonia', shows no appreciable difference in verse form from the preceding scene: the lines are still *versi sciolti*, and if anything have a less obvious poetic structure. This no doubt stems in part from Puccini's demands – mentioned earlier – for words to fit existing music; as the epigraph to this section suggests, these were at their most exigent in *pezzi lirici*. It is also interesting that here we find the first significant divergence between the printed libretto and the vocal score, suggesting that Puccini's verbal revisions continued to the very last moment. In the libretto, the first five lines of 'Recondita armonia' read:

Recondita armonia	7
di bellezze diverse! . . . E bruna Floria,	11
l'ardente amante mia,	7
e te, nobile fior, cinge la gloria	11
dell'ampie chiome bionde! . . !17	7

while in the vocal score the final two lines are condensed to:

e te, beltade ignota	7
cinta di chiome bionde! . . . 18	7

The change is representative: while the final version retains the central image ('cinta di chiome bionde'), it is more prosaic, realistic and immediate, telescoping the librettists' elaborate conceit into something more easily graspable, incidentally losing the original rhyme of Floria/gloria. In a sense, the alteration is emblematic. Puccini's desire for verbal immediacy led him to ignore that subtle interaction between verse forms and musical forms which had played so central a role in the work of Verdi and his predecessors. As a result, the libretto became at once more difficult to produce and less respectable as a literary genre. In the circumstances, it should surprise nobody that Giacosa spent so much of his time complaining.

Tonality and drama

Few would suggest that an opera such as *Tosca* is not a large-scale dramatic structure which in many ways has a perceptible unity of design; nor would many deny that it is a tonal work of art; yet the extent to which we are justified in linking 'drama' and 'tonality', to regard the two systems as capable of large-scale interaction, remains a matter of considerable debate. On a more local level, there is of course no doubt that tonal change and cross-reference can act as powerful forces for dramatic articulation; but from such small-scale detail, it is a large conceptual leap to the identification of a putative overall key structure such as we might find (indeed, might expect) in a symphonic work. To suggest the presence of a 'tonic' against which all other keys are heard as more-or-less remote is yet a further stage.

It is perhaps symptomatic of Puccini studies that, so far as his works are concerned, the problem has hardly been addressed; but with Verdi, a nearly comparable case in this as in many other respects, there exists a considerable range of opinion. We have on the one hand those such as Siegmund Levarie, who is happy to identify 'tonal flow' across an entire opera, and who can confidently state that *Il trovatore* 'begins in E major and ends in E flat minor, so that the tonal flow of the entire work amounts to an enharmonically reinterpreted Neapolitan cadence'.[19] What is more, Levarie can state this with an air of its being axiomatic, and offers 'proof' which, in the context of such broad assertions, often seems tangential or merely anecdotal. At the other extreme there is Julian Budden, whose unparallelled knowledge of Verdi's operas has led him to conclude that 'in accounting for the unity of a Verdi opera we cannot speak of tonal schemes since these operate when at all only within the compass of a separate number'.[20] Both authors have been criticized for their opinions, and it is clear that nothing like a consensus has yet been achieved. Perhaps answers will arise from a broader perspective. It is certainly interesting that, in an earlier contribution to this series of Opera Handbooks, Arnold Whittall is sceptical of finding such a tonal masterplan even in Wagner's *Parsifal*, a work evidently far more firmly grounded in the German symphonic tradition:

The fundamental importance of tonality in *Parsifal*, and the evident persistence of certain types of tonal relationships, notably the familiar nineteenth-century emphasis on chords and keys a third apart to open broader perspectives than those provided by emphasis on dominant and subdominant relations, seems to invite the proposal of some grand theory, not merely of tonal *usage*, but of tonal *unity*. *Parsifal* certainly coheres around tonal as well as thematic recurrences, and most of the principal tonal centres are found on the major or minor third axis around A flat. Yet it is difficult to regard the A flat major in which the work begins and ends, and which occurs from time to time during its course, as performing the kind of pivotal function that the tonic key of a symphonic structure performs: such 'monotonality' is as impracticable a concept in a music drama as it is in a number opera. [21]

In such an atmosphere of debate, it is best to speak straight out. I find no evidence for a governing structure of tonal motion in *Tosca*, nor even for a firm sense of tonal hierarchy within each act. The first act begins and ends with the same motif, for example, and a simple process of transposition turns the concluding statement, with minimum alteration, into an emphatic final cadence. The sense of closure, that one cycle of the drama has been completed, is immediately felt by the listener. But to suggest that the E flat major tonality thus emphasized is heard as the resolution of the act's entire harmonic motion – a motion which, as we shall see, is startling in its diversity – would be foolhardy. Puccini's tonal procedures, his preference for patterned juxtapositions of keys a third apart and his occasional repetition of a harmonic pattern notwithstanding, are more short-term, fundamentally because they are more pragmatic. The composer's habit of transposing sections of his operas up or down a step at a late stage of composition seems to confirm this attitude. In the autograph score of *La Bohème*, for example, a lengthy passage including the opening of 'Che gelida manina' is in C major, the key, incidentally, in which it is recalled in the final pages of the act. Puccini only decided to alter it to the definitive D flat major at a later date, after he had entrusted the score to his publisher Ricordi. [22] Such transpositions may, of course, have been effected precisely to form certain internal tonal relationships, although here the reverse seems to have been the case; but the stage of composition at which they occur does, I think, confirm that they were not amongst the composer's first, essential priorities.

Some specific examples from Act I of *Tosca* may clarify the position, simultaneously illustrating the unlikelihood of there being anything like 'monotonality', and examining the extent to which tonality and drama can be linked at the local level. The final section of the love duet between Tosca and Cavaradossi, beginning with the words 'Mia gelosa' (60/3/3–68/2/4), has a rather unusual key scheme. Its clear E major tonality (though arrived at via a Neapolitan chord from the previous E flat major section) is interrupted by a passage in F major. This whole section is thematically marked off by an extended statement of an important theme, that loosely identified with the love between Tosca and Cavaradossi:

Ex. 19

For several reasons we can be sure that the choice of this particular tonality was not merely casual. For one thing, the identification of E major with Ex. 19 has been prepared earlier in the act: our first hint of the theme, in the orchestral interlude which accompanies Cavaradossi's first entrance (14/2/2–3), is in that key, as is its next statement (again the orchestra), which coincides with Tosca's first off-stage words (32/3/1–3). There is also a more subtle cross-reference. In this tonality, the wide-spaced chords with which the love duet ends (68/2/1) cannot fail to remind us of the final chord of the 'Scarpia' motif which begins the opera and is so prominent a part of its musical fabric (1/1/1–3, etc.). In this way, arguably the two most important themes in the opera – themes which, taken together and given their most common semantic identification, encompass the 'fatal triangle' around which the plot revolves – are identified by tonal cross-reference, backed up by orchestral sonority and registral spacing.

The chromatic shift on to F major carries evident dramatic significance, not least in the actual moments of modulation. The first of these side-slips downwards in a manner which, at least to this listener, marks the passage as a slightly gauche first cousin to Wagner's love theme in Act I of *Die Walküre*. Musically it serves as a perfect illustration of a further facet of the eponymous heroine's character. We have already seen her as demurely religious, passionately jealous, and lightly flirtatious; now the words;

Dilla ancora
la parola che consola . . .
dilla ancora![23]

place her (for the first and only time in this act) as a more conventional operatic heroine, surrendering meekly to her lover's embrace.
The eventual move back to E major is also put to dramatic use, as it
allows a moment of tonal neutrality during which prosaic details of
the plot can be communicated in recitative style (a device Puccini
evidently favoured: see the end of 'Mi chiamano Mimì' from Act I of
La Bohème).

The F major section itself is controlled by Cavaradossi, allowing
him to reassert himself in preparation for the 'action' scene with
Angelotti which follows. We feel the achievement of F major to be
essentially for him, and the section is taken up by his solo reprise
of Ex. 19. Here the choice of tonality becomes crucial. While, in
E major, Ex. 19 comes to its climax on a comfortably climactic
high A (63/2/2), here it occurs on high B flat, a distinctive note in
the operatic tenor's range. Furthermore, the tonal placing of the
reprise refers the whole section back to Cavaradossi's earlier aria in
Act I, 'Recondita armonia' (19–26), with which it shares the F major
tonality, an insistence on high F as a pivotal vocal sonority, and a
climax on high B flat:

Ex. 20a

(23/2/3 – 24/1/1)

CAV.

To - sca_ sei tu!

Ex. 20b

(65/1/4 – 65/2/3)

CAV.

l'al - ma_ac - quie - ta, sem-pre "t'a - mo" ti_ di - rò!

A further factor also deserves mention. It is hard to doubt that the
high incidence in this repertoire of tenor arias in flat keys is not over-
whelmingly due to the fact that high B flat is the highest note which
a tenor can be relied upon to sing with security while still sounding in
love (as opposed to in pain or patriotic fervour),[24] or that these two

passages are not illustrations of the point. One could continue with other details which make the overall E major – F major – E major tonal plan of this section appropriate and resonant, but perhaps the point has been stressed sufficiently. Taken separately, none of the points *governs* the choice of tonality: the decision is fundamentally a pragmatic one, taken on the basis of an accumulation of detail rather than to suit any grand plan.[25]

A different, perhaps more typically Puccinian progression occurs in the passage leading up to Ex. 20a (12–19); typical in the sense that juxtapositions of keys a third apart are a common feature of his large-scale harmonic movements. As we can see from Ex. 21, the passage connecting the Sacristan's reciting of the *Angelus* to Cavaradossi's 'Recondita armonia', both of which are in F major, follows a broad plan of descending major thirds, with the first intermediate stage (D flat/C sharp) itself prolonged through a third-related key

Ex. 21

expansion (to E major). As we would expect, each new key marks a stage in the dialogue:

D flat major   : Cavaradossi mounts the dais and uncovers his picture;
E major   : He stares at it (and, the music suggests, thinks of Tosca);
C sharp major : The Sacristan describes the unknown woman who has served as the subject of the painting;
A major   : Cavaradossi continues the description;
F major   : Cavaradossi takes up his palette and continues with his painting.

The suitability of such progressions in music conceived primarily in vocal terms is clear, as the connecting threads between keys are typically pivot *notes* (rather than pivot *chords*), if necessary enharmonically reinterpreted. One might also point out that, as the upper line of Ex. 21 attempts to show, the bass progression away from F is complemented by a large-scale melodic ascent; and, most strikingly, that the outer F major sections are identified by their shared insistence on the note F as a dominating vocal sonority. Similar sections occur several times in Act I of *Tosca*, notably in the chorus which immediately precedes Scarpia's entrance (84/2/1–94/1/1), in which the move from A major to B flat major is embellished by a series of abrupt third juxtapositions; and in the *Andante mosso* section of the Scarpia–Tosca exchange (112/1/3–117/1/), where again, as in Ex. 21, a tonal centre is prolonged by an arpeggiation of its flattened third. Progressions such as these were used frequently by Verdi, and represent one of the clearest, least problematic areas of similarity between the two composers. But thoughts of some recent Verdi analysis immediately suggest that one add a note about possible transfer of structural levels. It might, for example, be tempting to relate the large-scale augmented triad progression in Ex. 21 to the whole-tone harmonies and augmented triads which are such a prominent feature on the harmonic surface of this opera. Tempting, that is, in theory only: if audibility were an important criterion, few would defend the notion in this particular case. As so often, it is a theoretical concept more honoured in the breach than the observance; abstractions of any kind have a way of sitting rather uncomfortably when applied to so patent a pragmatist as Puccini.

However much the examples above tend to suggest the outer limits of what may be termed 'tonal coherence' in a strict, functional sense, it is undeniable that broad variations of harmonic language serve to articulate large-scale structural elements of *Tosca*. The first act finds its basic structure from an alternation of 'action' and 'reflection' passages, and, as we can see, these are differentiated musically in part by harmonic means:

Characters	Harmonic type	Page nos.
1. Angelotti	Chromatic	1–7
2. Sacristan/Cavaradossi	Diatonic	7–29
3. Cavaradossi/Angelotti	Chromatic	29–36
4. Cavaradossi/Tosca	Diatonic	36–68
5. Cavaradossi/Angelotti	Chromatic	68–82
6. Sacristan/Chorus	Diatonic	82–94
7. Scarpia/Tosca	Chromatic	94–128
8. Scarpia/Chorus	Diatonic	128–144

Naturally, the terms 'chromatic' and 'diatonic' should be taken only in the most general sense: the large-scale 'chromatic' sections contain contrasting areas of diatonicism, and vice-versa; furthermore, overlaying this patterned alternation is a gradual movement towards diatonicism, with section 1 the most consistently chromatic, and section 8 the most consistently diatonic. There is also, of course, a parallel contrast on the rhythmic level, with the diatonic sections showing far more rhythmic stability, both at the phrase level and in larger periods.

Vague though it is, the distinction is useful in allowing us to categorize certain recurring features in Puccini's harmonic language. In the lyrical, diatonic sections perhaps the most obvious trait is a tendency to inflect the music flatwards, either with gestures towards the subdominant region, or by employing modal mixture. This occurs in a number of contexts. Sometimes it is merely a cadential feature, an injection of harmonic colour which at the same time relaxes the tension (25/3; 29/1; 49/2). Elsewhere it is used at more critical moments. It bites deeper into the heart of the music when vocal climaxes are underpinned (some might say undermined) by flatwards-inflected harmonies (44/3; 48/2; 60/1). On occasions we hear a melody which sinks to the extent of being accompanied by descending root position triads, as does Tosca's 'Ed io venivo a lui tutta dogliosa' (119/3ff), though this device is used far less frequently in *Tosca* than in the previous opera, *La Bohème*. On a slightly larger level, there are some set pieces which move so freely between a 'tonic' and 'subdominant' that it becomes difficult to establish the primary key centre (a particularly good example is the passage from the Sacristan's entry up to his singing of the *Angelus* (7–11), which at one point even touches on the subdominant of the subdominant).

The eschewing of tension is also achieved by Puccini's tendency to linger – sometimes altogether indecisively – on the submediant and/ or supertonic chords at moments of climax. Cavaradossi's final phrase in 'Recondita armonia', with its meandering bass line and high B flat supported by ii^7, is typical, as is the omission of the leading note (and hence of any tritone tension) in the subsequent dominant ninth chord (Ex. 22). In this sense the imposing finale to Act I gains its effect through the simplest of means: the ostinato which controls the section is, harmonically, little more than a continuous oscillation of ii^7/V^7 in E flat major.

Pentatonic writing, though it plays a less important part in this opera than in those which surround it (*La Bohème* and *Madama Butterfly*), is yet another method whereby Puccini manages to avoid tension but add harmonic colour. Again, the best example comes from 'Recondita armonia', in which the orchestral introduction (evidently intended to illustrate the stage directions: 'Cavaradossi paints

Ex. 22

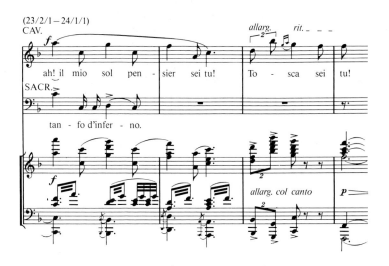

rapidly, stopping often to survey his work') is almost purely pentatonic. We might also recall that the cadence so commonly used in lyrical sections, ii⁷/ V⁹ (leading note omitted)/ I, uses, before the tonic chord, an exclusively pentatonic collection. Even the final arrival of the tonic chord is frequently coloured in a static manner, by placing it in second inversion. Examples abound (19/1–2; 64/3/2; 67/1/1; 84/2ff; 112/1/3ff); the range of context is considerable.

In the 'chromatic' sections of the first act, the surface of the music sounds very different, but on closer inspection we find that many of the recurring features mentioned above can also be found, albeit with different emphases and, often, a change from major to minor mode. A striking aspect of 'action' scenes, one which on the surface seem to differentiate them strongly from the 'reflection' scenes, is their prominent use of a particular seventh chord, the one made up of two minor thirds and a major third. The ubiquity of this, the so-called 'half-diminished' chord, in late nineteenth-century Italian operatic music is matched only by that of the diminished seventh chord some fifty years earlier, and one finds it frequently throughout Puccini's work. The 'jealousy' interlude in the Tosca–Cavaradossi duet, for example (50/2/2–57/3/4), which is a chromatic section embedded in a lyrical one, is structured around a succession of outbursts from the heroine, each more intense than the last, and each coming to a climax on this distinctive chord (Ex. 23a, b and c). But, as one can see from these examples, the potentially protean nature of the chord – its ability (like the diminished seventh) to resolve in a number of directions and hence into a number of possible keys – is

Ex. 23a

(51/3/3 – 52/1/1)

Ex. 23b

(53/3/4 – 54/1/2)

Ex. 23c

(55/3/1 – 3)

not exploited. In each case, the chord is treated in its most conventional, diatonic context in the minor mode, as a simple predominant seventh (ii⁷), and, no matter how much Puccini disguises the resolution with registral change, each dutifully resolves on to 'its' dominant seventh. In this sense, the chord may be heard as a minor-mode analogue of ii⁷ in the major, the repetition and function of which has been mentioned above. Though the sound is superficially different, the underlying harmonic syntax is identical.

Perhaps the most immediately obvious of the 'new' harmonic devices in *Tosca*, one which characterizes much of the chromatic writing in the opera, is the use of whole-tone harmony. The inverted commas round 'new' are justified even within the context of Puccini's work: as Spike Hughes has pointed out, the 'Scarpia' chords which begin the opera and are the most obvious generator of whole-tone writing occur (at the same pitch level and with an added scale step) in Act IV of *La Bohème*.[26] In retrospect, the descending whole tones in the earlier opera seem almost insolently enclosed within a tonal context by the perfect cadence which follows them (Ex. 24a and b). But naturally the context is all-important, and the parallel is above all useful as a means of reminding ourselves that whole-tone writing is not unique to *Tosca*. The extent to which the three 'Scarpia' chords

Ex. 24a *La Bohème*, Act IV

Ex. 24b

are aptly named will be discussed in the following section, as will its various reappearances in Act I; but, outside its immediate thematic context in Ex. 24b, the tritone juxtaposition embedded in the progression (B flat – E) does exert a certain influence. A sequence of descending tritones accompanies Angelotti's early moments on stage (2/3/4–3/2/1); later on, in the orchestral introduction to the second Cavaradossi–Angelotti dialogue, there is a more abrupt juxtaposition of chords a tritone apart (58/2/2–4). Returning to the opening, we might find an ambiguous reference to the harmonic goal of Ex. 24b in the fact that, on two occasions (5/1/5; 6/3/5ff), the music comes to rest on an unresolved second inversion seventh on E, decorated by chromatic neighbour chords.

There are broader applications: the manner in which (perhaps with Debussy's example) Puccini learnt to exploit the whole-tone possibilities of dominant ninth chords (the ninth chord in C major, for example, can have four adjacent whole tones: F–G–A–B); or how the 'Angelotti' theme (2/1/1ff) is, in the second half of the act, customarily curtailed to encompass chords a tritone apart (69/1–2; 74/3–4; 81/1/1–3; 108/3/3–109/1/1). But perhaps some special attention is due to three passages which, though they have little to do with the 'Scarpia' theme, nevertheless prolong whole-tone harmony in a manner which sounds strikingly modern. The passages have something in common dramatically: in the first, Scarpia meditates on how he can make use of Attavanti's fan (99/1/1–100/1/1); in the second, he presents the fan to Tosca (117/1/4–117/3/3); in the third, Tosca distractedly reacts to this 'proof' of her lover's infidelity (124/1/1–125/2/3). In each of the three cases, the whole-tone harmony is in the form of an augmented triad – in all but the first a static one; and each of these triads is then, with the minimum of alteration, treated as a dominant chord which resolves, in as clear a manner as possible, on to the 'correct' tonic. Like the half-diminished chord which acted in a diatonic context, and the pentatonic writing which was absorbed into a conventional cadence, we find that a surface radicalism hides a clear, conventional functionality. Though we have good reason to believe that Puccini was genuinely interested in his more radical contemporaries, their innovations rarely penetrated beneath the surface of his musical language.

Motif

A commentary on *Parsifal* concerned principally with motives would doubtless be able to present a formidably lengthy list of statements, derivations and transformations, in which interest would centre not only on the composer's promptness in responding to the clues implanted in his own text, but also on the commentator's ingenuity in noting possible connections. Yet it is not the mere presence of thematic material, whether obviously or deviously derived from a particular *Gestalt* or not, which is important, so much as the relationship of the musical and dramatic character of that material to the total context in which it appears.[27]

Arnold Whittall, in an essay already quoted from in this chapter, takes a firm position on the activity, sometimes rather grandly termed 'motivic analysis', in which commentators apply more-or-less precise semantic labels to recurring musical material. Elsewhere he states that: 'Music communicates most immediately and generally through the atmosphere its themes and textures create, and it is not the job of the analyst to interfere in this direct contact between composer and listener: his prime concern is with structure, not translatable meaning.' The fact that I find myself in broad agreement with Whittall on this matter, but can still devote a section of this chapter to 'motif', will not, I hope, be seen as necessarily a contradiction. In the case of Wagner such matters have been almost endlessly debated and, at least in recent times, have typically been approached with an air of humility: seeming anomalies are, it is assumed, more likely due to the listener's – rather than the composer's – blunted sensibilities. With Puccini there has been no such investigation, and no such consensus exists. In fact, critical confusion over the intention and scope of recurring themes presents one of the most considerable barriers in our path towards an understanding of the composer's attempts at musical drama.

Perhaps it is as well, in the circumstances, to begin by identifying the themes which recur in Act I of *Tosca*. Whatever difficulties arise in compiling such a list lie for the most part in the narrowness of Puccini's harmonic and melodic language (the former discussed in some detail in the previous section). When is a recurrence simply the repetition of some favourite cliché; when has an attempt been made to repeat a previous idea with the intention of alerting the listener to the cross-reference? In the end, decisions on such matters are personal; they depend on how keenly the desire to find unity and 'translatable meaning' is felt by the listener. I have tried to be as conservative as possible, only including material about whose intentional repetition there can be no argument. The self-imposed restriction to Act I turns out to be less inhibiting than one might assume: as so frequently with Puccini, the first act has by far the greatest variety of

musical invention. Nevertheless, a few famous recurrences have had
to be omitted, notably the appearance of the Act I love duet's opening theme (36/2/1ff) in Tosca's Act II aria 'Vissi d'arte' (243/3/1ff).
Even taking this into account, the final list is, at least by Wagnerian
standards, surprisingly small (Ex. 25a–m).

Ex. 25a

(1/1/1−3)

Ex. 25b

(2/1/1−2)

Ex. 25c

(2/3/4−2/4/1)

Ex. 25d

(4/1/1−3)

Ex. 25e

(5/1/3−5)

Ex. 25f

(7/1/1−4)

Ex. 25g
(8/2/3 – 8/3/2)

Ex. 25h
(14/2/2 – 3)

Ex. 25i
(19/3/2 – 20/2/1)

Ex. 25j
(30/1/1 – 30/2/2)

Ex. 25k
(32/1/2 – 32/2/1)

Ex. 25l
(34/1/1 – 2)

Ex. 25m
(37/2/1 – 38/1/1)

Any problems of selection, however, are slight in comparison with those which confront the commentator when he considers identification. It soon becomes clear that Puccini uses motifs in a manner which refers to a number of traditions. One is that of the Wagnerian *Leitmotiv*, though it is easy to overstress this particular line of descent: it is rare to find motifs combining in the seamless, often contrapuntal context so typical of mature Wagner. The orchestral introduction to Act II is perhaps an example, employing as it does subtle reminiscences from at least four previous ideas; but passages of such richness are the exception rather than the rule:

Ex. 26

More frequently the technique is that of Puccini's Italian antecedents, namely of the 'reminiscence motif', which returns as a discrete entity, rarely undergoes significant development, and typically underlines a dramatic or verbal cross-reference.[28]

But even reference to these three techniques is insufficient, as on occasions Puccini seems to disregard any previous association and employ themes as part of a purely musical structure. The results can be confusing, the interpretations difficult and not always to Puccini's credit. A most notorious example, one for which the composer has been frequently anathematized, is the reprise of 'E lucevan le stelle' in the final moments of the opera. Joseph Kerman's exasperation (see page 74) is easy to understand. The theme is that of Cavaradossi's soliloquy earlier in the third act; Tosca has had no opportunity to hear it; what we see and what we hear seem out of joint. As always, a number of ingenious explanations are available to the commentator; he might try as follows: the plot revolves around three characters, all of whom Puccini wishes to recall in these closing moments. Hence we *see* Tosca, the *words* refer to Scarpia (Tosca's final words are 'O Scarpia, avanti a Dio!'), and the *music* recalls Cavaradossi by means of his most extended aria. But few will be convinced by such an interpretation: its subtlety is quite at odds with the music, which in these closing moments is uncompromising in its blatancy. As Mosco Carner has pointed out, the overwhelming reason for the reprise has nothing to do with fine dramatic detail: it is done to leave the 'big' tune of Act III ringing in the audience's ears as the curtain falls.[29]

However, other cases of seeming inconsistency may not be so readily explained, nor necessarily rebound against the composer. Consider for example the opening theme of the opera (Ex. 25a). No one has any doubts about labelling this the 'Scarpia' theme (I have used the term as a convenient shorthand elsewhere in this chapter), and most of its appearances in Act I fall easily under such a rubric. Cavaradossi's venomous description of Scarpia is underpinned by a fivefold repetition of the theme (75/1/1–76/1/2); and Scarpia's own entrance is marked by a further four repetitions (94/1/1–96/1/1). With such prompting, the emphatic statements at the beginning and end of the act are easily understood as references to Scarpia's controlling influence over the action. The remaining two statements in Act I are, however, more problematical. The first marks Angelotti's success in finding the key to the Attavanti chapel (5/5/1–5); the second (in which the whole-tone descent is extended and filled-in) accompanies Cavaradossi's directions to a secret hiding place in the well near his villa (79/3/4–80/4/3). In both cases, the particular musical nature of the theme might seem programmatically appropriate, but in neither is the idea of Scarpia any more relevant than in a dozen other passages. Again, as with the reprise of 'E lucevan le stelle', we have to ignore the immediate dramatic relevance of the theme, and look instead at the larger musico-dramatic context. A glance at the list of 'chromatic' and 'diatonic' scenes (see page 136–7) shows that each of these statements occurs as a point of musical repose at the end of a section, and that each is followed by a further hectic reprise of the ubiquitous Ex. 25b, which is in turn interrupted by the start of a new section marked by the entry of the Sacristan and 'his' theme (Ex. 25f). In each case, the presence of Ex. 25a thus serves to underline musically a broad similarity between the endings of scenes; and this function temporarily over-rules its semantic identification. Although, in a sense, the theme *does* retain a certain identity: just as at the beginning and end of the act, it functions in these two instances as a 'cadence' of sorts, punctuating important structural moments in the drama with its all-embracing register and emphatic harmonic direction.

Ex. 25j is a further case in point. Its appearances in the Act I love duet ('Quella donna' . . . (38/2) and 'Quei passi' (54/3/2–55/1/2)) might tempt us to label it as a 'jealousy' motif. Indeed, its particular type of chromaticism is quite in keeping with the traditional musical symbol of this emotion in nineteenth-century Italian opera; the similarity to Iago's 'Temete, signor, la gelosia' in Act II of Verdi's *Otello* is, for example, unmistakable (Ex. 27). But in fact the initial

Ex. 27 *Otello*. Act II

IAGO:

Te - me - te, si - gnor, la ge - lo - si - a!

ppp

morendo

statements of this idea occur in the brief meeting between Cavaradossi and Angelotti which immediately precedes the love duet. There, it is a dominant musical image, its appearance at the beginning and end of the scene framing the action and, by its alteration of mode and dynamic, underlining the swift progression from triumphant recognition ('Voi! Cavaradossi!' (30/1/1–30/3/5)) to subdued parting ('Presto! . . . Grazie!' (35/1/4–35/3/3)). Its function is thus structural; it is only later, as Tosca repeats the idea when referring to her half-heard impression of the meeting, that it acquires an added layer of semantic richness, symbolizing not just one moment of jealousy, but the emotion itself.

Even with themes which seem indissolubly linked to a particular character or dramatic idea, it is dangerous to assume that Puccini will proceed with absolute consistency. Ex. 25g is clearly intended as one of the themes associated with the Marchesa Attavanti, Angelotti's loyal sister: each statement in Act I is accompanied by either a scenic or a verbal reference to her. But in Act II the link seems to have dissolved, and the theme accompanies Spoletta's description of Cavaradossi's contempt in the face of interrogation (159/3/3–160/2/4); the theme takes on a 'political' flavour only tangentially perceived in Act I. Ex. 25i is a further 'Attavanti' theme (it is plain that Puccini deemed her especially in need of clear and varied musical treatment, presumably because we have no opportunity to see her on stage); and this time it survives into Act II – see its skilful interpolation into the 'Ed or fra noi' duet (186/3/1–187/1/1). However, rigid adherence to the association would lead to curious assumptions. Cavaradossi's comparison of Attavanti and Tosca in 'Recondita armonia' ends with the words '. . . il mio solo pensier . . . Tosca sei tu!' ('. . . my only thought, Tosca, is you!'), but the instrumental coda to the aria features a reprise of the 'Attavanti' theme. Are we to assume that Cavaradossi has changed his mind? Clearly, such literalness is an absurdity. The theme is placed there for a musical reason, namely that its flatwards tendency is appropriate as a gentle postlude in which all sense of tension is avoided.

One could continue dissecting themes, but perhaps the point has been sufficiently stressed. Sooner or later, one must confront the obverse of the coin, and consider the extent to which all these themes may be organically related. The level at which an individual commentator will feel justified in suggesting derivations from one theme to another is a matter both of training and of the extent he feels organicism to be a necessary state for a musical drama. But the dangers of such an enquiry are manifest. There is what one might term an occupational hazard: that one's desire to reveal organic unity along symphonic lines will allow the eye to lead the ear. Thus, from a recent commentary, we read that:

While it would be too much to claim that Puccini was a cerebral composer of the order of Schönberg, he was a supreme musical craftsman, and part of his strength lay in his manipulation of these symbolic themes in a subtle and often complex relationship. If, for example, you take the top notes of the Scarpia sequence of chords, it forms a chromatic upward phrase [Ex. 25a]. Reverse this, expand it a little, and you have the theme which expresses the other side of his personality as shown at the start of the Second Act [Ex. 26].[30]

'Connexions' such as this are clearly inspired by previous semantic identification of themes rather than by audibility: ironically, the obvious audible connexion between these two passages – they both outline the tritone (Ex. 25a B flat – E; Ex. 26 G sharp – D) – is not mentioned.

A second danger is that, because of the narrowness of his musical world, Puccini sometimes seems to offer us an embarrassment of riches, a wealth of recurring features; as mentioned earlier, the boundary between what is 'organicism' and what the casual repetition of a personal cliché becomes virtually impossible to draw. Often, it is a matter of relative density: of comparing one opera with others, using the latter as 'controls'. A glance at Ex. 25, for example, shows that the perfect fourth is a prominent feature of many of the themes, whether as a direct interval (f, h, i, l) or with intermediate scale steps (b, g, j). The extent to which this observation is pertinent to *Tosca* (rather than to Puccini's predilection for this interval throughout his career) can only be revealed by examining with equal rigour the thematic material of *La Bohème*, *Turandot*, etc.; and the mere fact of such a perusal begins to undermine one's case. It is with some diffidence that one proceeds. Ex. 25a is a sequence of root position chords in which the relationship of the upper line to the root is: 3rd, 5th, tonic; the first three chords of Ex. 25b, the second musical idea of the opera, are also in root position, and there the upper line progression is: tonic, 5th, 3rd. The fourth chord of Ex. 25b, its initial harmonic 'goal', bears comparison with the progression which underpins the first statement of Ex. 25g, where identical pitch levels are retained in a different overall tonal context. And so one could continue through the list, but inevitably with a gathering sense that these relationships, if not casual, are hardly at the heart of the unity *Tosca* possesses.

The Italian critic Luigi Torchi, whose lengthy assessment of *Tosca*, though highly critical, still commands attention some eighty years after it was written, suggested that Puccini's treatment of motif was a product of rampant internationalism. He had adopted the Wagnerian *Leitmotiv*, but it had inevitably suffered from its cultural deracination and, '. . . in its new Italian home . . . does not work in the organism of the drama . . . it is a spectator, not an actor'.[31] While, following Whittall, we might disagree with Torchi's implied remarks on what constitutes the deepest structure of a Wagnerian music drama, we can only concur with his assessment as it applies to *Tosca*. Puccini's treatment of motif is a confused and confusing meeting-ground of traditions, sometimes highly effective, sometimes tautological, sometimes downright distracting; but above all we have the impression that the motif is externally applied, and remains tangential to the essential musical and dramatic continuity.

11   'Tosca' in the United States

BY WILLIAM ASHBROOK

The history of *Tosca* in the United States following its successful
introduction at the Metropolitan on 4 February 1901 has been one of
apparently unflagging popularity. A staple in the repertory of the
resident American companies, it has been nothing less in the offer-
ings of the various touring companies, such as the San Carlo, which
used to criss-cross the continent in fat times and lean. It seems safe to
assert that there must be scarcely a city or a town in the United States
where opera has been given in the last eighty years that has not been
exposed to at least one *Tosca*. Because of the nature of its plot and its
historic setting in well-known Roman monuments there has been
little temptation to produce *Tosca* in alien epochs or styles; conse-
quently the American history of *Tosca* tends naturally to focus upon
the many exceptional performers who have appeared in it.

   The first American cast of *Tosca* was headed by Milka Ternina as
Tosca, Giuseppe Cremonini (who had been the first des Grieux in
Puccini's *Manon Lescaut*) as Cavaradossi and Antonio Scotti as
Scarpia; the conductor was Luigi Mancinelli. With the exception of
the tenor, the principals and conductor were those of the Covent
Garden première the previous July, a sequence typical of the regime
of Maurice Grau that then dominated the principal opera houses of
both London and New York. This performance was reviewed by the
teutonically-oriented Henry Krehbiel in *The New York Tribune* with
obvious distaste, yet not without some effort at objectivity. 'What is
it like?' he asks. 'Much of it like shreds and patches of many things
with which the operatic stage has long been familiar. There are ef-
forts at characterization by means of melodic, harmonic and rhythmic symbols, of which the most striking and least original is the succession of chords which serves as the introduction to the first scene.'
He goes on to speak of 'phrases of real pith and moment . . . mixed
with painful reiteration and with all the color tints which Puccini is
able to scrape from a marvelously varied and garish orchestral

143

palette.' He had to admit, however, to 'the fluency of it all'. He gives little space to the performance, remarking with 'amazement' on Ternina's 'tragic power', which reminds him of that of Emma Calvé in Massenet's *La Navarraise*. He concludes his review by admitting that 'the sumptuous stage settings' along with the interpretations of Ternina and Scotti 'created unbounded delight'. Reviewing the same performance, W. J. Henderson in *The New York Times* took a more favourable attitude toward Puccini's music. 'His orchestration is always solid, picturesque, ingenious. He uses voices with the skill of an Italian. In short he is a gifted and well-trained composer . . .'

Both critics were put off by the seamier aspects of the opera's plot. But the public emphatically was not. The sensationalism of the subject proved a piquant attraction, and, from the first, audiences were intrigued by the opportunities the title role afforded a gifted singing actress. The villainy of Baron Scarpia as embodied by Antonio Scotti, a characterization regarded as classic, was to become an almost unvarying fixture at the Metropolitan, both in New York and on tour, until his retirement from the stage in 1933. When disability drove Ternina into premature retirement at the end of the following season, the role of Tosca was assumed by the American Emma Eames, a beautiful woman with a voice of ample proportions, but reputed to be a cool, detached actress. To contradict that last impression there are some excerpts dimly recorded at the Metropolitan by Lionel Mapleson of Eames's fourth performance of the part (3 January 1903); these reveal surprising glimpses of temperament and dramatic involvement. The following season the casting of *Tosca* was strengthened by the addition of Caruso as Cavaradossi, his third role at the Metropolitan. Over the next decade and a half, the company was favoured by the presence of a number of Toscas who brought a variety of apposite endowments to the role. There was the beautiful Lina Cavalieri, who had the advantage of Puccini's personal coaching as Tosca. On 22 November 1909 the variously gifted Geraldine Farrar first undertook the role, which was to become particularly associated with her. Three weeks after Farrar's first Tosca, the role was given to the imposing Olive Fremstad, whose mature interpretation afforded an interesting contrast to Farrar's more youthful characterization. Two years later a third impressive Tosca joined them when Emmy Destinn brought her vocal amplitude to the part. In 1916, to fill the gap left by Destinn's internment in Europe, Claudia Muzio made her New York début as Tosca, but the competition of the enormously popular Farrar kept the role from becoming a central one to Muzio's repertory in New York. The 1919/20 Metropolitan season opened on 17 November with *Tosca*, sung by Farrar, Caruso and Scotti, as much a tribute to their durability as to the work's continuing hold on the public. But if the days of this constellation were numbered, a new era for *Tosca* lay in the near future.

With the advent of Maria Jeritza for the 1921/2 season, *Tosca* took on a new lease of life. Deems Taylor began his review of her first New York appearance in the role, which took place on 1 December, by writing: 'No one who saw Tosca last night is soon to forget her.' With Farrar's retirement at the close of that season, Jeritza assumed a scarcely challenged proprietorship of the role that lasted for her tenure with the Metropolitan, and her success as Tosca is reflected in an increased number of performances of Puccini's opera. Aureliano Pertile launched his brief American career the night of Jeritza's first Tosca, but she was most frequently partnered by Giovanni Martinelli, while Scotti remained the apparent *sine qua non* as Scarpia. When Jeritza left the Metropolitan in 1932, *Tosca* entered upon lean years.

It was revived occasionally, Lotte Lehmann and Marjorie Lawrence failing to win the public with their versions, while Dusolina Giannini and Maria Caniglia proved more plausible although they appeared in it only briefly, and it was not until Grace Moore first sang her communicative, if erratic, Tosca at the Metropolitan in 1941 that a singer there could demonstrate much dominance over the role. After Moore's untimely death in an aircrash, *Tosca* once again lacked a soprano who could make the role her own.

That void was filled when the role was first assumed at the Metropolitan by Renata Tebaldi in March 1955. Tebaldi's was a seasoned performance, for she had been singing Tosca since October 1946, and her vocal and personal allure proved sufficient to convince New York audiences that they were once again in the presence of the real thing. The fortunes of the opera were further strengthened when Zinka Milanov introduced the Metropolitan to her Tosca the following December. Yet undoubtedly the most unforgettable Tosca of the post-World War II years in New York was Maria Callas, first seen there on 15 November 1956. And this impression was produced on the basis of only six appearances there as Tosca: four between 1956 and 1958 and two in 1965.

Tosca has not, of course, been the exclusive property of the Metropolitan in New York. A notable production was that opening Hammerstein's Manhattan Opera Company for its third season, when his forces essayed Puccini's score for the first time. On that occasion Cleofonte Campanini conducted, Maria Labia made her American début, and Giovanni Zenatello appeared as Cavaradossi, while Scarpia was the exemplary Maurice Renaud. *The New York Sun* on 10 November 1908 described that performance as 'fiery' and appreciated Labia more as an actress than as a singer. The *Tribune* reviewed the same performance and singled out Renaud for special praise, calling his interpretation 'free from every melodramatic element in action, finely eloquent in its diction'. At the fifth performance at the Manhattan that season, Lina Cavalieri made her debut with this company, and Mario Sammarco sang Scarpia. *Tosca* returned to the Manhattan the following season – Hammerstein's final one in New York before being bought out by the Metropolitan – when it served for the American debut of one of the best equipped singers, both vocally and dramatically, to appear in the role in New York, Carmen Melis.

While *Tosca* owed its first introduction at a number of major American cities to the tours of the Metropolitan – Philadelphia, Boston and Chicago, for instance – it early appeared in the repertories of local resident companies, once they were established. For example, the Boston Opera Company first gave it on 7 March 1910, when it was sung by Celestina Boninsegna, the tenor Florencio Constantino and the baritone Georges Baklanoff. Boninsegna cannot have made a favourable impression as Tosca, for in the remaining three performance of the opera that season she was replaced by the practically forgotten Fely Dereyne. The following year Carmen Melis joined the Boston company, and Tosca was one of her admired parts. At her Boston début in the role she was partnered by the tenor Jadlowker and by Baklanoff, the conductor being Roberto Moranzoni. The final *Tosca* of the 1911–12 Boston season was exceptional in that it was conducted by Felix Weingartner, and the title role was sung by his third wife, Lucille Marcel. If Scotti and Renaud had been the finest Scarpias heard as yet in America, this Weingartner performance added a third to that number, Vanni Marcoux. The following year Mary Garden introduced her sensationally acted Tosca to Boston, in a performance in which the three principals – Charles Dalmorès was Cavaradossi, Marcoux the Scarpia – sang their parts in French. It is strange, indeed, that Garden who performed this role many times in America, always used the French translation (except for the aria'Vissi d'arte', which she invariably sang in the original Italian), even when the others appearing with her used the original text.

When the Chicago Opera Company opened for its first season,

that of 1910/11, the eighth opera to be performed there was *Tosca*. On this occasion it was sung by Janina Korolewicz-Wayda, the tenor Amadeo Bassi and Sammarco. The other three performances by the company that season featured different sopranos: Farrar, Lillian Grenville and Melis. The second Chicago season was one of the few *Tosca*-less ones in the company's history. In the third, Mary Garden introduced her Tosca to Chicago – Boston had already heard it – when the opera was next given there in January 1913. There was great demand to hear her in the part as rumours of her uninhibited acting in the second act in Boston, a display that caused the mayor of that city to threaten to ban the opera, had whetted anticipations. When Vanni Marcoux joined the Chicago troupe for the 1913/14 season, he made his debut as Scarpia on the opening night, appearing with Garden. In succeeding years in Chicago the most notable Toscas were Rosa Raisa, Yvonne Gall and Claudia Muzio, the last having left the Metropolitan in 1922 to join the Chicago company. The final season of the Chicago Civic Opera, that of 1931/2, opened with *Tosca*, which was sung by Muzio with Jan Kiepura making his American debut as Cavaradossi and Marcoux as Scarpia; Moranzoni conducted.

When the Chicago Lyric Company was constituted in the autumn of 1954, its initial repertory included *Tosca*, first sung on 18 November with Eleanor Steber, Giuseppe di Stefano, and introducing to American audiences the magisterial Scarpia of Tito Gobbi. Although Callas appeared in Chicago that season and the following one, Tosca was not one of her parts there. In October 1956, *Tosca* returned, now with Tebaldi and Jussi Bjoerling joining Gobbi. Gobbi has since produced *Tosca* for Chicago and has coached Scarpias at the Metropolitan in that role.

When the San Francisco Opera Company gave its inaugural season in the autumn of 1923, *Tosca*, sung by a cast including Bianca Saroya, Martinelli and Giuseppe de Luca, formed part of the repertory. The following year saw Muzio and Gigli being threatened by de Luca's Scarpia. In 1926 Muzio's companions in *Tosca* there were Antonio Cortis (Cavaradossi) and Marcel Journet (Scarpia). When the War Memorial Opera House was opened on 15 October 1932, the inaugural work was *Tosca*, with Muzio now being abetted by Dino Borgioli as Cavaradossi and Alfredo Gandolfi as Scarpia. Of this performance there exists an air-check of Act I, a precious souvenir of Muzio's potency as Tosca. Of the later Toscas in San Francisco, none of them made as strong an impression as Dorothy Kirsten, who sang the role in four 'editions', two of them honoured as opening nights.

The general popularity of *Tosca* in the United States is as easily explicable as it is in the rest of the opera-producing world. Engrossing as theatre and set to memorably apposite music, it belongs to that class of works that the general public finds enhanced by familiarity. The vividness of the opportunities it affords the protagonists and antagonist makes the comparisons of how this Tosca matches that in her handling of the 'business' at the end of Act II, or how this Cavaradossi or that delivered 'E lucevan le stelle', a topic for endless conversations.

Notes

1 Sardou and his *La Tosca*

1   Sardou's most important plays were *La Tosca*, *Théodora*, *Madame-Sans-Gêne*, *Cléopâtre*, *Fédora*, *Thermidor* and *Dante*.

2 Naturalism in opera: verismo

1   Compare this with what Strauss said to Josef Gregor, the librettist of his *Daphne*: 'Nothing must take place off-stage, not even the killing of Leukippos. Theatre and not literature!'
2   In a letter to Ricordi, 20 November 1880. Appendix to *Copialettere* (Milan, 1913), p. 559.
3   Compare La Harpe's saying about Gluck's *Alceste*: 'Tous les arts sont fondés sur des conventions, sur des données. Quand je viens à l'opéra, c'est pour entendre la musique. Je n'ignore pas qu'Alceste ne faisait ses adieux à Admète en chantant un air; mais comme Alceste est sur le théâtre pour chanter, si je retrouve sa douleur et son amour dans un air bien mélodieux, je jouirai de son chant en m'intéressant à son infortune' (All the arts are based on conventions, on given assumptions. When I go to the opera, it is to hear music. I am aware that Alceste did not pay farewell to Admète by singing an air; but, since Alceste is on-stage in order to sing, if I find her sorrow and her love in a well-turned air, I shall enjoy her song, thus becoming interested in her misfortune (La Harpe, 'Sur la musique théatrale', in *Oeuvres*, vol. 5 (Paris, 1820), p. 154).
4   From a speech to the Congrès Scientifique held at Aix-en-Provence in 1866, in which Zola surveyed the development of the novel from the earliest Greek specimens to the nineteenth century. Quoted from F. W. J. Hemmings, *Emile Zola* (London, 1953).

3 Genesis of *Tosca*

1   Fontana was a writer and journalist who adhered to the tenets of *la scapigliatura* (literally 'the dishevelled ones'), a somewhat eccentric literary movement which flourished in Italy in the 1860s and 1870s, and which propagated non-conformism in the arts and showed preference for foreign authors as against native talent. Hence Fontana's choice of an apparently Slavonic legend mentioned by Heinrich Heine as the sub-

149

ject for *Le Villi* and of *Edgar*, after a book-drama by Alfred de Musset. For the same reason he suggested Sardou's *La Tosca* to Puccini. The head of this short-lived movement was Arrigo Boito who, significantly, chose not an Italian subject but Goethe's *Faust* as material for his first opera libretto *Mefistofele*. The musical members of the dying *scapigliatura* were Puccini, Mascagni, Leoncavallo and Franchetti.

2 *Carteggi pucciniani*, ed. Eugenio Gara (Milan, 1958), Letter 31.

3 Lucio D'Ambra, *Vite dei musicisti*, quoted in George Marek, *Puccini* (London, 1952), p. 175.

4 This passage was in the original of Debussy's *Monsieur Croche antidillettante* (Paris, 1921) but was suppressed in *Monsieur Croche et autres écrits*, ed. François Lesure (Paris, 1971) as too scathing of Italian veristic operas (see Preface, p. 14).

5 The original French text reads: Puccini et Leoncavallo prétendent à l'étude de caractère, voire même à une sorte de psychologie brutale qui n'aboutit, en réalité, qu'à de la simple anecdote.

   Les deux *Vies de Bohème* en sont des examples frappants. Dans l'une la dureté d'un fait divers où la sentimentalité a ce nasillement spécial aux 'canzones napolitaines'. Dans l'autre, si M. Puccini essaie de retrouver l'atmosphère des rues et des âmes parisiennes, ça fait tout de même un bruit italien. Je n'aurais pas la prétention de lui reprocher d'être italien, mais pourquoi diable avoir choisi *La Vie de Bohème? (Gil Blas,* 16 February 1903).

   ('Puccini and Leoncavallo pretend to study character, even a kind of brutal psychology which actually ends only in mere anecdote.

   Of this the two *Vies de Bohème* are striking examples. In the one both the harshness of the slice of life and the sentimentality have the peculiar nasal sound of Neapolitan songs. In the other, even though M. Puccini attempts to reproduce the street atmosphere and the souls of Parisians, it still sounds like an Italian noise. I would not dare to reproach him for being Italian, but why the devil has he chosen *La Vie de Bohème*?')

   Strangely enough, Debussy did not comment on *Tosca* which, I assume, he did not see when the opera was first produced in Paris in October 1903.

6 Quoted in Mosco Carner, 'Debussy and Puccini', in *Major and Minor* (London, 1980), pp. 140–1.

7 See Mosco Carner, *Puccini. A Critical Biography* (London, 2nd edn 1974), pp. 271–82.

8 Gino Monaldi, *Giacomo Puccini* (Rome, n.d.), p. 48. According to Monaldi, Verdi then went on to tell him the changes he had in mind, but unfortunately Monaldi, beyond saying they were 'most beautiful', did not record them.

9 Quoted in Marek, *Puccini*, p. 170.

10 *Carteggi pucciniani*, Letter 169.

11 From a letter of 6 July 1896, quoted in Piero Nardi, *Vita e tempo di Giuseppe Giacosa* (Milan, 1949), p. 763.

12 *Carteggi*, Letter 169.

13 Nardi, *Giacosa*, p. 765.

14 Letter of 9 September 1898, quoted ibid., p. 767.

15 Between 1903 and 1906 Sardou offered Puccini three more of his plays for an opera. There are a round dozen operas and operettas based on Sardou, the most important of which are Johann Strauss's *Carnival in Rome*, based on *Piccolomini*, and Giordano's *Fédora* and *Madame-Sans-Gêne*.

16 Arnaldo Fraccaroli, *La vita di Giacomo Puccini* (Milan, 1925; 2nd edn 1957), p. 109.

17 He later published his memoirs – Pietro Panichelli, *Il 'pretino' di Giacomo Puccini racconta* (Pisa, 3rd edn 1949) – a garrulous little book, which gives interesting details about the composer's private life and some valuable insights into his mind.

18 *Carteggi*, Letter 195.

19 The manuscript score suggests that Puccini began the composition of Act III with Cavaradossi's aria.

20 Almost exactly the same thing occurred with Michele's great monologue towards the end of *Il tabarro*, which was originally a philosophical meditation on the River Seine and at the composer's special request was transformed by Adami, his librettist, into an expression of murderous jealousy. 'I want to finish with a "muoio disperato"', the composer wrote to Adami.

21 Vincent Seligman, *Puccini among Friends* (London, 1938), p. 44.

22 The man indirectly responsible for 'tutta Roma' was not Puccini but the Mayor of Parma. When Puccini visited the city its mayor made it a point of honour to show him the sights. Coming to the monument that Maria Luisa had had erected in memory of her second husband, Count Neipperg, who had ruled Parma with a firm hand, the mayor said, 'There is a remembrance in marble of the man before whom trembled all Parma.' Struck by this pithy phrase, Puccini entered it in the libretto, changing 'whole city' into 'all Rome'. See Claudio Fratta Cavalcabò, *Puccini e Mascagni* (Parma, 1942), p. 12. I am indebted to Dr Costantino Garosi of Venice for kindly sending me a photocopy of the relevant pages of the book.

23 According to entries in the manuscript score, the orchestration of Act II was completed on 16 July 1899 and that of Act III on 27 September.

24 *Carteggi*, Letter 208.

25 Ibid., Letter 209.

4 Synopsis

1 *Bohème* and *Turandot* also begin with a motto-theme.

2 At this point Angelotti's earlier *marcatissimo* theme enters on the low flutes *p*, Puccini evidently identifying the unknown woman (Attavanti) with her brother.

3 The scoring here is noteworthy for its beauty: the melody (*dolcissimo*) lies on the flute and is doubled at the distance of two octaves by the cellos while the rest of the upper strings play arpeggios *pizz.*, suggesting a large harp. At the repeat of the section the scoring is reversed: the first violins now have the melody while the upper woodwind play the harp-like arpeggios.

4   As before, the entry here of the 'Angelotti' motif (Ex. 2a) suggests that Puccini identifies the Attavanti with her brother.
5   The same device is used by Marie in Act I, sc. 3 of Berg's *Wozzeck*, to shut out the sound of a passing military band.
6   The reason for this strange command is given in Sardou. Scarpia does not want it to be known that Angelotti has escaped his clutches by poisoning himself, and wants to make it appear that he has been arrested and hanged by the Chief of Police in the course of his duty (see also Ch. 5, n. 6).

5 Play and opera: a comparison

1   *More Opera Nights* (London, 1954), chapter on *Tosca*, pp. 187–252.
2   *Literature as Opera* (London, 1979), p. 367.
3   *More Opera Nights*, pp. 204ff.
4   Sardou's date is in strict accordance with historical events. On the morning of 14 June the Austrians under General Melas attacked the French at Marengo and, due to their superior artillery, forced them to withdraw. Melas returned to his headquarters at Alessandria, leaving General Zach in command. Zach, instead of pursuing the French as he had been ordered by Melas, paused to consolidate his troops. Just before the French retreat Napoleon had arrived on the battle-field; the French forces regrouped, advanced and beat the Austrians, with heavy losses. The next morning Melas concluded an armistice. It must be assumed that the false report of his victory over the French reached Rome early in the morning of 17 June and that the news of Napoleon's victory was received on the afternoon or evening of that day.
5   In 1919 the French composer Georges de Seyne attempted an unsuccessful imitation of *Tosca* in his two-act *La Mafia*, in which the leader of this secret society plays a role similar to that of Scarpia.
6   This was done at the express wish of Lady Hamilton (a close friend of the Queen), whose lover Angelotti had been in London a long time before – an affair about which he had been rather indiscreet. Lady Hamilton wants to see him hang in Naples. Tempting as it would be to relate this episode in full, it is unnecessary for our purpose. I have only alluded to it as a typical example of Sardou's dramatic device of linking historical personages with fictitious events.
7   Apart from the similarity of the two names, there are some striking points of contact in the life-story of the two men. Liborio Angelucci (1746–1811) was one of the first Romans to sympathize with the ideas of the French Revolution. He was arrested by the authorities and thrown into the Castel Sant'Angelo where he was said to have attempted suicide. When the French occupied Rome in 1798, Angelucci was freed and made Consul of the new Roman Republic; but after its fall in September 1799 he had to flee and could not return to Rome until 1811. Unlike Sardou's Angelotti, however, Angelucci died a natural death. I am indebted to Jürgen Maehder of Bern University for drawing my attention to the article on Angelucci in the *Dizionario biografico degli Italiani* (Rome, 1960–   ), pp. 251–3.

6 First production and critical history

1   Being a realistic opera in which, moreover, the drama is fixed to a definite historical place and time, *Tosca* allows little room for experimental productions such as have been seen more recently in some romantic and symbolist operas like *Der fliegende Holländer* and the *Ring* at Bayreuth and *Pelléas et Mélisande* at the London Coliseum. In a recent *Tosca* production by the Scottish Opera the time of the action was brought forward to the last months of Mussolini's regime in 1943, with Scarpia and his henchmen as Blackshirts and Tosca appearing in the last act in a black raincoat and a beret resembling a present-day guerrilla. This of course made the subject of the opera more topical, but I wondered by what stretch of the imagination the producer reconciled his up-dating with the fact that Napoleon's battle at Marengo took place in 1800. I have also seen a televised performance of *Tosca* produced in Rome in which the only novelty was the fact that the action took place in the actual historical localities in which the drama is set. Interesting though it was, this attempt at strict authenticity added nothing to the dramatic impact of the opera. See also p. 143.

2   Mascagni, Franchetti, Cilea and such declared enemies of opera as Martucci and Sgambati.

3   Puccini declared Jeritza his best-ever Tosca and 'one of the most original artists'. It was Jeritza who, at the Vienna Staatsoper, accidentally introduced the half-lying position in which some singers of Tosca address their 'Vissi d'arte' to Scarpia. In her tussle with the lustful Chief of Police she had, during a rehearsal, slipped to the ground; Puccini, who was present, considered this position so perfectly in keeping with the emotional situation that he asked her to retain it. In my student days in Vienna I saw Jeritza in *Tosca* many times. It was not until summer 1984 that I saw at Covent Garden a Tosca (Maria Zambieri) who again sang 'Vissi d'arte' in that position which added considerably to the emotional impact of the aria.

4   Herman Klein, *The Golden Age of Opera* (London, 1933), p. 253.

5   'Eine ganz famose Aufführung nach jeder Richtung, dass man ganz paff ist, so etwas in einer österreichischen Provinzstadt zu finden. Aber das Werk! Im ersten Akt Aufzug des Pabstes zu fortwährendem Glockenge-bimmel das eigens von Italien bestellt werden musste, – 2. Akt wird einer mit grässlichem Schreien *gefoltert*, ein anderer mit einem spitzi-gen Brotmesser erdolcht, – 3. Akt wird wieder mit der Aussicht von einer Zitadelle auf ganz Rom riesig gebimbambummelt, wieder eine ganz andere Partie Glocken – und Einer von einer Compagnie Soldaten durch Erschiessen hingerichtet.

     Vor dem Schiessen bin ich aufgestanden und fortgegangen. Man braucht wohl nicht zu sagen, dass das Ganze wieder ein grosses Meister-machwerk ist; heutzutage instrumentiert jeder Schusterbub famos.' Alma Mahler, *Gustav Mahler, Erinnerungen und Briefe* (Amsterdam, 1940), p. 281. English edn, ed. Donald Mitchell (London, 1969), p. 225. (*Meistermachwerk* is an ingenious conflation of two compound words: *Meisterwerk* (masterpiece) and *Machwerk* (bungled piece or con-coction).)

6   Fausto Torrefranca, *Giacomo Puccini e l'opera internazionale* (Turin, 1912), p. 54.
7   It is worth noting that the renaissance of English music started, partly, from similar premises and about the same period.
8   Ildebrando Pizzetti, *Musicisti contemporanei. Saggi critici* (Milan, 1914), pp. 130ff.
9   Pizzetti's first opera, *Fedra*, to a libretto by d'Annunzio, dates from 1915. He also set T. S. Eliot's *Murder in the Cathedral* to music (1968).
10 Joseph Kerman, *Opera as Drama* (New York, 1956), pp. 252.
11 Ibid., p. 255.
12 Ibid., p. 254.
13 Ibid., pp. 17–20.

8 Style and technique

1   See Hans-Jürgen Winterhoff, *Analytische Untersuchungen zu Puccinis 'Tosca'* (Regensburg, 1973), p. 25ff.
2   In Glinka (*Russlan and Lyudmila*, 1842) and Dargomizhsky (*The Stone Guest*, 1869) the whole-tone scale is linked with the supernatural, the strange and the demonic. It is an artificial scale probably constructed by Glinka.
3   It abounds independently or in conjunction with the whole-tone scale in *Butterfly*, *La fanciulla del west*, *Turandot*, and is also conspicuous in *Wozzeck*.
4   From the German point of view, *sinfonismo* has never been a strong suit of Italian composers. This is admitted by Claudio Cassini in his *Giacomo Puccini* (Turin, 1978), p. 247. In the strict Italian sense, *sinfonismo* simply means writing for orchestra. Thus Puccini's *Capriccio sinfonico* (1883) is a brilliant piece for orchestra but the symphonic element is largely confined to its title. His only genuinely symphonic piece is the orchestral intermezzo in the second act of *Butterfly*.
5   It may be doubted whether the 'Cavaradossi' theme (Ex. 4a) is really his or the Attavanti's; the second time we hear it is when Angelotti refers to 'my sister' and Cavaradossi exclaims, 'the Attavanti!'
6   The orchestral Interlude between Acts II and III of *Manon Lescaut* and Butterfly's short aria before committing suicide are in this 'dark key' (Beethoven). Significantly, the point at which Mimì dies in Act IV of *Bohème* is exactly marked by the entry of a quite unexpected B minor chord, after D flat major.

9 Musical and dramatic structure

1   It is an interesting coincidence that Hugo Wolf's Mörike song 'Auf ein altes Bild' shows an archaism achievéd by similar harmonic progressions.
2   André Coeuroy in *La Tosca de Puccini, Etude historique et critique* (Paris, 1923), p. 115.
3   The manner of her entrance is a specifically Puccinian device. Tosca announces her arrival, first, by her voice off-stage (her call 'Mario!',

repeated four times) before she enters the stage, exactly as is the case with the first appearance of Mimì and Musetta in *Bohème* and Cio-Cio-San in *Butterfly*. The device, apparently of impressionist origin, is based on the fact that we urgently wish to *see* the person whose voice we have heard in the distance or off-stage. By withholding immediate gratification of this wish Puccini generates a measure of tension so that our wish grows more urgent and the character's entrance more dramatic.

4 *Cf* the close of Acts I and III of *Manon Lescaut* and Musetta's waltz in Act II of *Bohème*.

5 Pietro Panichelli, *Il 'Pretino' di Giacomo Puccini racconta* (Pisa, 3rd edn 1949), p. 95.

6 It is likely that Puccini took a hint for this from the final scene in *Otello* in which the double basses play a conspicuous role.

10 Analysis: Act I in perspective

* It is a pleasure to acknowledge the assistance of several colleagues. William Ashbrook, Joanna Greenwood, David Lawton, Harold Powers and Arnold Whittall all read earlier drafts of the present chapter; their comments and criticisms have been most helpful; though final responsibility for the text of course remains with me, I am in their debt concerning a host of issues, both large and small.

1 For details of the critical reaction to *Tosca*, see p. 68ff.

2 Fausto Torrefranca, *Giacomo Puccini e l'opera internazionale* (Turin, 1912), p. vii.

3 Igor Stravinsky and Robert Craft, *Dialogues and a Diary* (London, 1968), p. 58.

4 Joseph Kerman, *Opera as Drama* (New York, 1956), p. 19.

5 Alec Harman and Wilfrid Mellers, *Man and his Music* (London, 1962), pp. 799-802; William Austin, *Music in the 20th Century* (London, 1966), pp. 107-10; Donald Jay Grout, *A Short History of Opera*, 2nd edn (New York and London, 1965), II, pp. 441-5.

6 See, for example, Claudio Sartori, ed., *Giacomo Puccini* (Milan, 1959); Mosco Carner, *Puccini. A Critical Biography*, 2nd edn (London, 1974). Also of interest is Hans-Jürgen Winterhoff, *Analytische Untersuchungen zu Puccinis 'Tosca'* (Regensburg, 1973), and Antonio Titone, *Vissi d'arte. Puccini e il disfacimento del melodramma* (Milan, 1972), the latter a bizarre but occasionally revealing attempt to apply structuralist methods to Puccini criticism.

7 Eugenio Gara, ed., *Carteggi Pucciniani* (Milan, 1958), p. 170.

8 Letter from Verdi to Ghislanzoni, dated 17 August 1870. Gaetano Cesari and Alessandro Luzio, eds., *I copialettere di Giuseppe Verdi* (Milan, 1913), pp. 641-2.

9 For this purpose, one must consult a libretto which preserves the original layout of the text: too frequently, modern editions fail in this respect, and thus obscure the distinctions between various verse forms. A happy exception is the series of English National Opera Guides, ed. Nicholas John (London, 1980-   ). *Aida* is no. 2 in the series (1980), *Tosca* is no. 16 (1982).

10   For a detailed example of the interaction of words and music in nineteenth-century Italian opera, see Pierluigi Petrobelli, 'Music in the Theatre (à propos of *Aida*, Act III)', in James Redmond, ed., *Themes in Drama 3: Drama, Dance and Music* (Cambridge, 1981), pp. 129–42.

11   RAMFIS: He is young and brave – Now I will carry the God's decrees to the King. RADAMES: If I could be that warrior! If my dream could come true!. . . An army of brave men led by me. . . and the victory – and the praise of all in Memphis! – And, my gentle Aida, to return to you decked with laurels. . . To say to you: I have fought for you and I have won for you!// Heavenly Aida, divine form, mystical garland of light and flowers; you are the ruler of my thoughts, you are the splendour of my life.

12   TOSCA: Mario! CAVARADOSSI: I am here! Tosca: Why closed? Cavaradossi: The Sacristan wished it. Tosca: To whom were you talking? Cavaradossi: To you! Tosca: You were whispering to another. Where is she? Cavaradossi: Who? Tosca: She!. . . That woman!. . . I heard hurried steps and the rustle of a dress. Cavaradossi: Dreams! Tosca: You deny it? Cavaradossi: I deny it and I love you! Tosca: Oh! before the Madonna. First let me offer flowers and pray to her.

13   'Ah!. . . At last!. . . In my mad terror I saw the faces of spies in everyone. The basin. . . the column. . . 'At the foot of the Madonna' wrote my sister. . . Here is the key. . . and here the chapel!. . .'

14   'Of that unknown woman who has come here in these last days, full of devotion and piety.'

15   The numbers in parentheses, here and elsewhere, refer to the page number/ system number/ bar number (within system) of the current Ricordi vocal score of *Tosca*, plate number 109916.

16   SACRISTAN: (Away, Satan, away!) CAVARADOSSI: Give me the paints!

17   'Mysterious harmony of contrasting beauties!. . . My ardent love Floria is dark, and you, proud flower, encircled with the glory of your rich blond locks!. . .'

18   'and you, unknown beauty, encircled with blond locks!. . .'

19   Siegmund Levarie, 'Key Relations in Verdi's *Un ballo in maschera*', *19th–Century Music*, II (1978), p. 143.

20   Julian Budden, *The Operas of Verdi*, 3 vols. (London, 1973, 1978, 1981), I, p. 40.

21   Whittall's essay forms the third chapter of Lucy Beckett's Cambridge Opera Handbook *Richard Wagner: Parsifal* (Cambridge, 1981).

22   See William Ashbrook, *The Operas of Puccini* (London and New York, 1968), p. 65.

23   'Say it again, the word that consoles. . . say it again!'

24   See Jay Nicolaisen, *Italian Opera in Transition, 1871–1893, Studies in Musicology, No. 31* (Ann Arbor, 1980), p. 41.

25   Ashbrook, *Operas of Puccini*, pp. 70–1, suggests from his study of the autograph that this E major section of the duet may have been Puccini's initial inspiration, as it is on separate sheets. If this is the case, then the suggested 'chronology' for the cross-relations I mention will of course be reversed.

26 Spike Hughes, *Famous Puccini Operas* (London, 1959), p. 75.
27 Whittall, in Beckett, *Parsifal*, p. 63.
28 As many commentators have pointed out, Cavaradossi's 'Amaro sol per te' (Act III: 309/2/2ff) is taken from the original version of *Edgar*; such 'self-borrowing' is yet another aspect of Puccini's attitude to motif.
29 Carner, *Puccini*, pp. 377–8. See also Ch. 8, pp. 115–16 above.
30 Bernard Keeffe, 'The Music of Puccini's *Tosca*', in Nicholas John, ed., *Tosca* (English National Opera Guide 16) (London, 1982), p. 17.
31 Luigi Torchi, 'Tosca', *Rivista musicale italiana*, VII (1900), p. 93.

Select bibliography

Adami, G. and Carner, M. (eds). *Letters of Giacomo Puccini*, London, 1974

Ashbrook, W. *The Operas of Puccini*, London and New York, 1968

Carner, M. *Puccini. A Critical Biography*, London, 1958, rev. edn 1974

Cassini, C. *Giacomo Puccini*, Turin, 1978

Chop, M. *Die Tosca*, Leipzig, 1924

Coeuroy, A. *La Tosca de Puccini. Etude historique et critique*, Paris, 1923

Gara, E. (ed.). *Carteggi pucciniani*, Milan, 1958

Greenfield, E. *Puccini: Keeper of the Seal*, London, 1958

Hughes, S. *Famous Puccini Operas*, London, 1959

Korngold, J. *Die romanische Oper der Gegenwart. Kritische Aufsätze*, Vienna, 1922

Newman, E. *More Opera Nights*, London, 1943, 2nd edn 1954

Sartori, C. *Puccini*, Milan, 1959

Winterhoff, H.-J. *Analytische Untersuchungen zu Puccinis 'Tosca'*, Regensburg, 1973

There have so far been only three monographs on *Tosca* but the opera is dealt with in all comprehensive biographies of Puccini, of which I have listed the most important, and in every opera guide.

Discography

BY MALCOLM WALKER

all recordings are in stereo unless otherwise stated

T Floria Tosca
C Mario Cavaradossi
S Baron Scarpia

ⓜ mono recording
ⓔ electronically reprocessed stereo
④ cassette version

1918 Remondi *T*; Broccardi *C*; Zani & Fregosi *S*/chorus & orch/Sabajno
   La Voce del Padrone R or S
   5583–4, 5586, 5588, 5590–2, 5594–6, 5598, 5600, 5602–4, 5606

1920 Bartolomasi *T*; Salvaneschi *C*; Pacini *S*/chorus/Milan SO/Sabajno
   La Voce del Padrone R or S
   5701–2, 5704, 5706, 5708–10, 5712–14, 5716, 5718, 5720–2, 5724

1929 Melis *T*; Pauli *C*; Granforte *S*/La Scala Chorus & Orch, Milan/
Sabajno   Discophilia ⓜ KS10/11

1930 Scacciati *T*; Granda *C*; Molinari *S*/La Scala Chorus, Milan SO/
Molajoli   Columbia D14594/14607
   CBS (US) ⓜ EL4

1938 Caniglia *T*; Gigli *C*; A. Borgioli *S*/Rome Opera Chorus & Orch/De
Fabritiis   EMI ⓜ 3C 153 00667–8M
   Seraphim ⓜ IB6027

1951 Guerrini *T*; Poggi *C*; Silveri *S*/RAI Turin Chorus & Orch/Molinari-
Pradelli   Cetra ⓔ LPO2055

1951 Dall'Argine *T*; Scattolini *C*; Colombo *S*/Vienna Academy Chorus,
Vienna State Opera Orch/Quadri
   Eurodisc ⓔ XD 27677 R

1951 Petrova *T*; Ruhl *C*; Campolonghi *S*/Maggio Musicale Fiorentino
Chorus & Orch/Tieri   Remington ⓜ 199–62

1952 Tebaldi *T*; Campora *C*; Mascherini *S*/Accademia Nazionale di Santa
Cecilia Chorus & Orch, Rome/Erede
   Decca ⓔ ESC206–7
   Richmond (US) ⓜ RS62002

1952   (live performance – Palacio de Bellas Artes, Mexico City) Callas *T*; Di Stefano *C*; Campolonghi *S*/Chorus & Orch of Palacio de Bellas Artes/Picco   Cetra ⓜ LO41

1953   (in German) Martinis *T*; Schock *C*; Metternich *S*/North West German Radio Chorus & Orch, Hamburg/Schuchter
                Eurodisc ⓜ 300 727 420

1953   Callas *T*; Di Stefano *C*; Gobbi *S*/La Scala Chorus & Orch, Milan/De Sabata   EMI ⓔ SLS824 ④ TC-SLS 824
                Angel ⓜ 3508BL

1955   Frazzoni *T*; Tagliavini *C*; Guelfi *S*/RAI Turin Chorus & SO/Basile
                Cetra ⓜ LPC1261

195?   (live performance – Metropolitan Opera House, New York) Kirsten *T*; Barioni *C*; Guarrera *S*/Metropolitan Opera Chorus & Orch/ Mitropoulos   Metropolitan Opera
                Record Club ⓜ MO724

1955   (live performance – Metropolitan Opera House, New York) Tebaldi *T*; Tucker *C*; Warren *S*/Metropolitan Opera Chorus & Orch/ Mitropoulos   Paragon ⓜ DSV52 003
                Metropolitan Opera
                Record Club ⓜ METIO

1956   Milanov *T*; Björling *C*; Warren *S*/Rome Opera Chorus & Orch/ Leinsdorf   RCA (Europe) VLS43535
                RCA (US) VICS6000 ④ V82–1022

1957   Stella *T*; Poggi *C*; Taddei *S*/Teatro di San Carlo Chorus & Orch, Naples/Serafin   Philips ⓜ 6720 007

1957   Olivero *T*; Fernandi *C*; Colombo *S*/RAI Turin Chorus & Orch/Tieri
                Discocorp ⓜ RP514

1959   Tebaldi *T*; Del Monaco *C*; London *S*/Accademia Nazionale di Santa Cecilia Chorus & Orch/Molinari-Pradelli
                Decca GOS612–3
                London OSA1210 ④ OSA5–1210

1959   Tebaldi *T*; Di Stefano *C*; Gobbi *S*/La Scala Chorus & Orch, Milan/ Gavazzeni   CLS ⓜ AMDRL22813

1960   (in French) Rhodes *T*; Lance *C*; Bacquier *S*/Paris Opera Chorus & Orch/Rosenthal   Véga 28017–9

1960   (in German) Woytowicz *T*; Kónya *C*; Borg *S*/Berlin State Opera Chorus, Berlin Staatskapelle/Stein
                DG SLPM138722–3

1962   Price *T*; Di Stefano *C*; Taddei *S*/Vienna State Opera Chorus, VPO/ Karajan   Decca 5BB123–4 ④ K59K22
                London OSA1284 ④ OSA5–1284

1964   Callas *T*; Bergonzi *C*; Gobbi *S*/Paris Opera Chorus, Paris Cons. Orch/Prêtre   EMI SLS917
                Angel SBL3655 ④ 4X2X–3655

1966   Nilsson *T*; Corelli *C*; Fischer-Dieskau *S*/Accademia Nazionale di Santa Cecilia Chorus and Orch, Rome/Maazel
                Decca JBD42001 ④ KJBCD42001
                London 42001

1967 (in Russian) Milashkina *T*; Andzaparidzye *C*; Klenov *S*/USSR Academy Chorus, USSR SO/Svetlanov
                                        Melodiya SM02315–19
1972 Price *T*; Domingo *C*; Milnes *S*/John Alldis Choir, Wandsworth School Boys' Choir, New Philharmonia Orch/Metha
                                        RCA GL20105
                                        RCA (US) ARL2–0105
1976 Vishnevskaya *T*; Bonisolli *C*; Manguerra *S*/French National Chorus & Orch/Rostropovich   DG 2707 087 ④ 3370 008
1976 Caballé *T*; Carreras *C*; Wixell *S*/Royal Opera House Chorus & Orch, Covent Garden/Davis   Philips 6700 108 ④ 7699 034
1976 Milashkina *T*; Atlantov *C*; Mazurok *S*/Bolshoi Theatre Chorus & Orch, Moscow/Ermler   EMI 3C 165 99357–8
1977 Zeani *T*; Fanateanu *C*; Herlea *S*/Boys' Choir, Rumanian National Opera Chorus & Orch, Bucarest/Trailescu
                                        Electrecord ST-ECE01412–4
1978 Freni *T*; Pavarotti *C*; Milnes *S*/Wandsworth School Boys' Choir, London Opera Chorus, National PO/Rescigno
                                        Decca D134D2 ④ K134K22
                                        London D12113 ④ 5–12113
1979 Ricciarelli *T*; Carreras *C*; Raimondi *S*/Schoenberg Children's Choir, German Opera Chorus, Berlin PO/Karajan
                                        DG 2707 121 ④ 3370 033
1980 Scotto *T*; Domingo *C*; Bruson *S*/St Clement Danes School Choir, Ambrosian Opera Chorus, Philharmonia Orch/Levine
                                        EMI SLS5213 ④ TCC-SLS5213
                                        Angel DSX3919
1983 Te Kanawa *T*; Aragall *C*; Nucci *S*/London Opera Chorus, National PO/Solti   London/Decca (awaiting release)

Index

162